Demonstrategy

Also by H. L. Hix

POETRY

Rain Inscription *
American Anger *
I'm Here to Learn to Dream in Your Language *
As Much As, If Not More Than *
First Fire, Then Birds *
Incident Light *
Legible Heavens *
God Bless *
Chromatic *
Shadows of Houses *
Surely As Birds Fly
Rational Numbers
Perfect Hell

TRANSLATIONS

Juhan Liiv, *Snow Drifts, I Sing: Selected Poems*, trans. with Jüri Talvet
Eugenijus Ališanka, *from unwritten histories*, trans. with the author
Jüri Talvet, *Of Snow, of Soul: New Selected Poems*, trans. with the author
Jüri Talvet, *Estonian Elegy: Selected Poems*, trans. with the author
Juhan Liiv, *The Mind Would Bear No Better*, trans. with Jüri Talvet
On the Way Home: An Anthology of Contemporary Estonian Poetry, trans. with Jüri Talvet
Jüri Talvet, *A Call for Cultural Symbiosis*, trans. with the author
Eugenijus Ališanka, *City of Ash*, trans. with the author

ANTHOLOGIES

Uncoverage: Asking After Recent Poetry
There's This Place I Know...
Ley Lines
Made Priceless: A Few Things Money Can't Buy
New Voices: Contemporary Poetry from the United States
Wild and Whirling Words: A Poetic Conversation *

THEORY AND CRITICISM

Lines of Inquiry *
As Easy As Lying: Essays on Poetry *
Understanding William H. Gass
Understanding W. S. Merwin
Spirits Hovering Over the Ashes: Legacies of Postmodern Theory
Morte d'Author: An Autopsy

* Also published by Etruscan Press

"Poetry is not dying for want of an audience; humanity is dying for want of poetry."

In the age when everything has a price tag, Hix explores and exposes the polarity of poetry. The book takes us on a journey deep into the beast of humanity, the underbelly of civilization, the core and foundation of what makes/marks us as humans and beasts. It's a book of paradox, riddles, exploration, play, and imagination.

What does poetry do? Nothing and everything, like air, water, soil, like birds, fish, trees, like love, spirit, our daily words… It lives within and without, all the time, and we are too often oblivious of this gift. It's a poet's job to bring this gift out and back, this gift that makes us human again.

Two thousand years ago, Confucius told his son who whined about having to study and write poetry every day: "Without poetry, how do we live?"

Hix's *Demonstrategy* goes further: our humanity and civilization needs poetry to survive and thrive. Everything may be tagged with a price, but not poetry.

—Wang Ping, author of *Ten Thousand Waves*

In his ambitious and learned study of poetry, H. L. Hix proposes a new poetics, ethopoetics, for a new posthuman world. Rather than a poetry of privatization, with its emphasis on exceptionalism and the enclosure of intellectual gain, he calls for an "implicationist" art that, by valuing hybridity and difference, can speak to all. The strategy's daemon is a generative spirit that erects no monuments, but broadens like a field of interactive root systems. Rilke's admonition, "You must revise your life," becomes valid, both for poetry and citizens of the Anthropocene. Hix is especially trenchant on poetry's uses of ambiguity: "Poetry, by embracing the paradox in which language is immersed, works *with* the language rather than *against* it." Poetry is a moral force, never demanding a final statement of truth, but rather enacting truth's complexity. *Demonstrategy* confirms that poetry *does* matter; indeed, it is central to our lives.

—Paul Hoover, author of *The Book of Unnamed Things*

Demonstrategy

Poetry, For and Against

H. L. Hix

Etruscan Press

Etruscan Press
Wilkes University
84 West South Street
Wilkes-Barre, PA 18766
(570) 408-4546

www.etruscanpress.org

Published 2019 by Etruscan Press
Printed in the United States of America
Cover image: Victor Babu, *Untitled*, 1990, Porcelain, black slip/glaze and resisted sprayed glazes, Collection Nerman Museum of Contemporary Art, Johnson County Community College, Overland Park, Kansas
Cover design by Lisa Reynolds
Interior design and typesetting by Todd Espenshade
The text of this book is set in Minion Pro.

First Edition

17 18 19 20 5 4 3 2 1

Library of Congress Cataloguing-in-Publication Data

Names: Hix, H. L., author.
Title: Demonstrategy : poetry, for and against / H.L. Hix.
Description: First edition. | Wilkes-Barre, PA : Etruscan Press, 2019. |
   Includes bibliographical references.
Identifiers: LCCN 2018015477 | ISBN 9780999753415
Subjects: LCSH: Poetics.
Classification: LCC PN1042 .H52 2019 | DDC 808.1--dc23
LC record available at https://lccn.loc.gov/2018015477

Please turn to the back of this book for a list of the sustaining funders of Etruscan Press.

This book is printed on recycled, acid-free paper.

Table of Contents

Article 9: One word changes, one word changes everything.

Article 10: Not yet as it should be, no longer as it was.

Acknowledgments

Before this inquiry was one, it was many.

Of those several inquiries, various were tentatively voiced, some at conferences (the "Poetic Ecologies" conference in Brussels, the national conferences of ASLE, MLA, and AWP, the conference of the Estonian Association of Comparative Literature, the "Hybrids, Monsters, and Other Aliens" conference in London, the "Under Western Skies" conference in Calgary, the "Flow and Fracture: the Ecopoetic Avant Garde" conference in Brussels, and the "Wit, Scholar, Mentor" conference in Austin), some as lectures (at Virginia Wesleyan University, Chulalongkorn University, the Université Libre de Bruxelles, and the University of Kansas). I thank my gracious hosts and interlocutors at those venues, especially Franca Bellarsi, Chad Weidner, Josh Weinstein, Lucile Desblache, Robert Boschman, Surapeepan Chatraporn, Jüri Talvet, Katre Talviste, and Gene Fendt. A few of these inquiries enjoyed first lives as lectures at Fairleigh Dickinson University's low-residency MFA program, and I am grateful to the members of that vibrant community.

Also, versions of individual inquiries were provisionally ventured in print, in these vehicles: *At Length* (6.1); *Comparative Critical Studies* (10.2); *Interlitteraria* (1.1, 5.1, 10.1); *Likestarlings* (1.2); *Making Poems*, ed. Todd F. Davis and Erin Murphy (8.1); *On Rhyme*, ed. David Caplan (9.1); *Poems and Their Making*, ed. Philip Brady (8.2); *Until Everything Is Continuous Again*, ed. Jonathan Weinert and Kevin Prufer (4.2); *Voltage Poetry* (6.2); AWP *Writers Chronicle* (2.1, 7.1); and *The Yale Review* (3.2). I am indebted to the editors of those publications for their intellectual nurture.

I am grateful yet again for Phil Brady's sage editorial counsel.

Demonstrategy

H. L. Hix

Preamble

I intend the coinage *demonstrategy* to break two ways, toward two pretended etymologies. As *demon strategy*, this book's title derives from *daimon*, the ancient Greek word for a divinity, genius, attendant spirit, and *strategía*, Greek for generalship, decision, command. As *demonstrate-gy*, it derives from the prefix *de-* and the root *monstrare*, the Latin verb meaning to show.

Both derivations imply that poetry, like a magnetic field, has two poles, in poetry's case one pole affirmative, the other oppositional.

The derivation from *daimon* poses the question Wittgenstein asked in this way: "Is this the sense of belief in the Devil: that not everything that comes to us as an inspiration comes from what is good?" It marks the tendency, in origin stories about poetry, to personify poetry's affirmative pole as a benign being, a god or angel or muse, and its oppositional pole as a malign being, a devil, as when Czeslaw Milosz grants that "poetry is rightly said to be dictated by a daimonion," but adds the disclaimer that "it's an exaggeration to maintain that he must be an angel." As a demon strategy, is poetry animated by a demon like the one that secured Socrates from error, or like those that gave the Gerasene to break all chains and fetters? This book's answer to that either/or is *yes*, to both.

The derivation from *monstrare* also offers an either/or. Does poetry demonstrate in the affirmative sense, as a lab experiment might demonstrate that one element can bond with another, and as a mathematical proof might demonstrate that the square of the length of one side of a right triangle equals the sum of the squares of the lengths of the other two sides? Or does it demonstrate in the oppositional sense, as workers in a union might demonstrate against unfair employment practices, and as affected citizens might demonstrate against an unjust political decision? Again, this book's answer to the either/or is *yes*, to both.

Thus the double entendre in the subtitle: that poetry itself ever urges both a for and an against, and that the book gives both a case for poetry and a case against it. That, because "for" and "against," also, each has more than one meaning. "For" here, to mean both in favor of, as in "I'm for gun control," and in service of, as in "the car is for getting back and forth to work." "Against," to mean both opposed to, as in "I'm against fracking," and adjacent to, as in "the ladder is against the wall."

Do the articles that follow explore poetry's polarities, or do they expose poetry's polarity? I hope the answer is *yes*.

Article 1:
Make another world, make this world otherwise.

1.1: Poetry Against Growth

One take on contemporary life sees technology as having displaced poetry, rendering it irrelevant or at best compensatory. On this view, we live in the information age, under the sign of Moore's Law, and poetry, as Wittgenstein observed even before digital supplanted analog, "is not used in the language game of giving information." Absence from popular culture confirms poetry's reduction to insignificance. Gaming and film and television reach billions worldwide, and generate billions in revenue; poetry reaches a tiny, tenuous, negligible audience, and operates at a loss, propped up by patronage, burdening rather than bolstering economic growth.

Consider, though, this contrary view: technology's influence makes poetry more urgent than ever, so urgent that it conditions the continued survival of the human species. Exclusion of poetry from popular culture symptomatizes not *poetry's* illness but *culture's*. Poetry is not dying for want of an audience; humanity is dying for want of poetry. In Charles Bernstein's words, we suffer "not the lack of mass audience for any particular poet but the lack of poetic thinking as an activated potential for all people." In fulfillment of that contrarian understanding, as a response to our want of poetry, I propose *ethopoesis*. The ethopoetic would recognize the urgency, even the *necessity*, of poetry, and envision a poetry adequate to this cultural need.

Technology and economy now enmesh the globe in ways, and to a degree, beyond precedent. Transportation has overcome regional limitations to the movement of goods; digital technology has overcome the limits distance once imposed on communication; corporations now enjoy worldwide market reach; resources from any region are accessible to exploitation by entities in distant regions; and so on. The economy has raced toward total globalization, but cultures and concepts of citizenship have lagged, remaining local and sectarian. Corporations have become thoroughly multinational, but political institutions remain stubbornly national; natural resources and manufactured products move easily from one place to another, but movement of humans is tightly restricted by national boundaries; those with capital find safety and security for their *money* more readily than those without capital can find safety and security for their *persons*; and so on.

This disparity between a global economy and local cultural and civic values has as one upshot structural violence: violence, as Paul Farmer puts it, perpetrated "by the strong against the weak, in complex social fields" in which "historically given" and "economically driven" conditions guarantee "that violent acts will ensue." Political democracy cannot be had without economic democracy; cultural and civic values must also check, not only be checked by, economic forces. Farmer does not identify poetry as an ally, but poetry urges, and furthers, the revaluation for which he calls. Until we construct, and enact, a global *culture* and global *citizenship*, our global *economy* will only be destructive: exaggerating the disparity between rich and poor, exhausting resources and generating waste faster and faster, prompting ever more terrorism and war and genocide.

Among the many ways to articulate why this is so, Janet Dine's is especially lucid. Capitalism, she affirms, in its essence is simple, and its primary tool, the contract, is functional and ethically sound. But "like any other human institution it [contract] can be corrupted," and the dominant contractually-based institutions, namely multinational corporations (e.g. banks) and international financial institutions (e.g. the IMF), have been corrupted. In a market economy, commercial law ought to allocate risk, but, Dine observes, it has not done so equitably. Instead, both international and national laws, "written," Dine reminds us, "mostly by wealthy élites," have participated in creating poverty the results of which include: more than one in eight humans is undernourished; one in eight humans does not have access to safe drinking water; two in five do not have access to adequate sanitation. That combination of factors kills 1.4 million children every year (4,000 children every day, one child every 20 seconds). In creating laws about contracts, commercial law establishes rules defining and protecting property, regulating how it is acquired and disposed of, but Dine emphasizes that "property rights are not rights over *things* but, on the contrary, rights against other people," specifically the right to *exclude* them. Laws constructed by and for those who already own property will pursue "the widest concept of property and freedom to trade" without regulatory control, inviting "accumulations of property without imposing countervailing responsibilities."

Dine depicts the global economy as not merely *out of step with*, but *dependent upon the suppression of*, valid conceptions of global culture and citizenship. Such an exposition suggests a condition for any suitable response. To mitigate the structural violence of our economy, we need cultural and civic parameters able to stand up to, and to modify, economic activity. Without what I call here the "ethopoetic," our attempts even to envision, much less to implement, such parameters cannot but be impoverished and futile. That impoverishment and futility is revealed by contrasting the medium of economic exchange with the medium of cultural and civic exchange. Along at least one vector, the contrast is stark. The medium of economic exchange, currency, homogenizes and distorts value. It makes everything fungible: by means of it, anything can be rendered equivalent to anything else. So many tons of rice equivalent to, and traded for, one automobile; so many hours of a person's labor at a certain job for one month's rent on an apartment. The medium of cultural exchange, language, recognizes value in its full variety and particularity. Its differentiating capacity enables it to resist and to limit fungibility, to preserve uniqueness from equivalence.

Currency performs its generalizing by substituting price for value, a substitution that erases any distinction between price and value. Currency, in other words, pretends that price *just is* value. Only in a medium other than currency can the substitution of price for value be challenged. Identifying language as such a medium grounds an apology for poetry, and proposes an ideal for poetry. That is, it explains why poetry is necessary and what poetry at its best might be.

In *Lyric Philosophy*, Jan Zwicky recognizes language's capacity for challenging the substitution of price for value, by proposing a way of seeing that she calls "lyric comprehension," which "does not distinguish between a thing's being and that-it-is-valuable." Lyric comprehension, by maintaining a thing's being as integral to its valuation, contrasts with pricing, which performs its valuation by substituting a uniform measure for a thing's being. Lyric comprehension opposes the economic comprehension manifest through currency. Zwicky extends this idea in *Wisdom and Metaphor*, invoking "ontological attention," a sister to lyric comprehension, as "a response to particularity: *this* porch, *this* laundry basket, *this* day." Because its object "cannot be substituted for, even when it is an object of considerable generality ('the country', 'cheese', 'garage sales')," ontological attention "is the antithesis of the attitude that regards things as 'resources', mere means to human ends." That the object cannot be substituted for means that its value has been preserved in distinction from price, which makes anything substitutable for anything else. In contrast to the voracious equivalences imposed by price (a $1,000 porch = any hundred $10 laundry baskets), *this*ness insists that no porch can substitute for this basket, no basket for this porch. Such linguistic and literary comprehension pushes back against the homogenizing imposed by economic comprehension.

The capacity of language to retain the uniqueness of a thing as integral to its identity and the being of a thing as integral to its valuation, is a *capacity*, one we can realize effectively or not. Which suggests an ideal for poetry: to fully realize the particularizing capacity of language, its resistance to the economic substitution of price for value. The ideal receives elegant formulation in Wysława Szymborska's Nobel Prize acceptance: "In daily speech," she says, "we all use phrases such as 'the ordinary world', 'ordinary life', 'the ordinary course of events.'" But in poetry, which realizes the particularizing capacity of language by weighing every word, "nothing is usual or normal. Not a single stone and not a single cloud above it. Not a single day and not a single night after it. And above all, not a single existence, not anyone's existence." In Szymborska's terms, nothing is usual or normal; in Zwicky's terms, nothing can be substituted for. Either way, poetry resists the global economy's pressure to make anything substitutable for anything else, and thus to make *everything* susceptible to market exchange.

Technology and economy have changed our *world*, but they also have changed *us*. We live in different circumstances than ever before, and we ourselves are different. Humanist and posthumanist accounts concur in the assessment that our reach now exceeds our grasp, and that this exceeding is not the unqualified, heavenly good that Browning's Andrea del Sarto sought.

Martha Nussbaum formulates the difference elegantly in her humanist manifesto *Not for Profit*. In our world, she declares, "people face one another across gulfs of geography, language, and nationality. More than at any time in the past, we all depend on people we have never seen, and they depend on us." Our most pressing problems are global, with no hope of solution "unless people once distant come together and cooperate in ways they have not before." The global economy "has tied all of us to distant lives. Our simplest decisions as consumers affect the living standards of people in distant nations" and "put pressure on the global environment." To some small extent, it was ever so. Hunter-gatherers pressured other species, and left a rubble of tools and shelters. A northerner's cotton blouse in the antebellum U.S. subsidized the enslavement of an African-American on a plantation down south. The difference in degree, though, is now so great as to amount to a difference in kind. My shoes subsidize child labor in Singapore, the car I drive sanctions the circumstances in which female factory workers are routinely raped and killed at the U.S./Mexico border, my trash is dumped into a vast dead zone in the Pacific, and on and on. Nussbaum finds it irresponsible of us "to bury our heads in the sand, ignoring the many ways in which we influence, every day, the lives of distant people." Until I reckon with that influence, my human interactions will be "mediated by the thin norms of market exchange in which human lives are seen primarily as instruments for gain," and I will continue to harm distant others.

If Nussbaum's humanist manifesto emphasizes the synchronic extension of our reach, its expansion across space, Timothy Morton's posthumanist manifesto *Hyperobjects* emphasizes the diachronic extension of our reach, its expansion across time. Morton distinguishes, as the fields through which our reach has come to extend, three timescales, "the *horrifying*, the *terrifying*, and the *petrifying*." The horrifying is the scale of five hundred years, beyond the time of Shakespeare's *Henry VIII* to the time of the events the play depicts, "historical" even to Shakespeare. Morton notes that I participate now in activities that will affect humans as far into the future as Henry VIII is in the past: "75 percent of global warming effects will persist until five hundred years from now." As at the "horrifying" timescale, so at the "terrifying" timescale of thirty thousand years. This is the distance into the past of the Chauvet Cave paintings, yet my current actions will have effects that far into the future: 25 percent of the carbon compounds my car releases the next time I drive to the market will remain in the atmosphere thirty thousand years from now. Even at the timescale Morton calls the "petrifying," my effects will linger: "7 percent of global warming effects will still be occurring," and "form built structures (skyscrapers, overpasses, garnets for lasers, graphene, bricks)" will have created "a layer of geological strata."

Morton's point is that "the future hollows out the present." Because it *can* be imagined, infinite duration — eternity — is forgiving. Because it *can't* be imagined, time at the scales Morton considers, the time of "very large finitude" rather than of infinity, is unforgiving. Morton describes us as participating in the construction of "hyperobjects" such as global warming, the very large finitude of which starkly reveals the degree by which my reach exceeds my grasp. Even my most trivial-seeming decisions/actions affect others far into the horrifying, terrifying, and petrifying futures: "A Styrofoam cup will outlive me by over four hundred years."

Changed circumstances and changed selves entail changed responsibilities. My indirect actions now are more potent than my direct actions; the unintended consequences of my actions always and necessarily exceed the intended consequences. The asymmetry between effect and control has switched. When others' effects on me exceed my control (the old situation) the result is tragedy: *my* destruction looms. For the Greek tragedians, my agency is inadequate to my circumstances (a fact personified as Fate, Necessity, and so on): my effects are too *small* to fulfill my intentions. For us, now, my agency is *over*adequate: my effects are too *large* for my intentions to manage. Now that my effects on others exceed my control (the new situation) the result is disaster (war, climate change, structural violence): *our* destruction looms. The state in which contemporary technology and the contemporary global economy have placed us differs from the "state of nature" Hobbes depicts. In Hobbes, we are *each* threatened with destruction: any human might be destroyed. In current circumstances, we are *all* threatened with destruction: humanity might be destroyed. In Hobbes, the bind is the prisoners' dilemma: we need a way to *remove* agency from the individual. Now the bind is Midas's touch: we need a way to *restrain* the agency of the individual.

This inversion of the relationship between agency and volition invites a contrast between the ethopoesis I am advocating, and the prevailing cultural norm, which I'll label *ethotechne*. Pairing Smokey Bear's familiar "Only YOU can prevent forest fires" with the invented correlative "Only YOU can prevent global warming" will advance the contrast, because of a difference between the two admonitions. Intent on fulfilling the first admonition, I will diligently monitor my decisions and actions when I go camping this year, and as a result of that diligence I will cause no forest fires. There will be one forest fire less than otherwise there might have been. Even if I am equally intent on fulfilling the second admonition, though, there is no due diligence for me to perform. I can take measures to reduce my carbon footprint, but global warming will continue inexorably, not measurably or discernibly slowed. My part in forest fires differs from my part in global warming, and the difference between the two exemplifies the difference between ethotechne and ethopoesis.

In ethotechne, my intention governs my agency: I can, for example, cause a forest fire by myself. In contrast, in ethopoesis my intention does not govern (is not adequate to) my agency. I cannot cause global warming by myself. In the ethotechnical realm, intention and effect converge; in the ethopoetic realm, they diverge. Consequently, in the ethotechnical, teleological and deontological approaches to ethical concerns will tend to concur, and in the ethopoetic, they will tend to contrast. My having good intentions will suffice in relation to forest fires, because those intentions, since they govern my agency, will yield effects consonant with the intentions. My having good intentions will not suffice in relation to global warming, because, absent their governing my agency, effects consistent with them need not attend them. In ethotechne, my intention and agency relate to one another in such a way that I can decide *not* to cause a forest fire, but in ethopoesis, my intention and agency relate to one another differently: I cannot simply decide *not* to cause global warming.

Primary to ethotechne is *occasion*: I can start a forest fire only when I am on a camping trip, *in* the forest, not when I am at home in the city. In ethopoesis, though, *conditions* are primary. I live in a time period and within a human social arrangement in which hydrocarbons are the primary energy source, as a result of which carbon is being released into the atmosphere faster than it can be absorbed by natural processes. It is not a specific occasion on which I cause global warming; it's the conditions in which I move and live that cause global warming. I might wake up one morning and decide that the time is right to set a forest fire. There is no *occasion*, though, for my bringing about global warming: I am engaged in doing so continually, not occasionally.

The forest fire can be described in a clear and adequate way by a simple causal chain. I decide to leave a campfire burning when I'm not watching it, or I carelessly throw a cigarette butt out the window of my car as I drive through Yellowstone; that action lights dry leaves on fire and that fire expands into a large area. I do one particular thing, from which follows another particular thing. In ethopoesis, though, the cause/effect relationship is not a simple causal chain, but a complex causal network. It's not that I, or any single human, decided to burn hydrocarbons as a primary energy source, but that many things (the invention of the internal combustion engine, the mass production of motor vehicles, the burning of coal for energy, and so on), various decisions made by various people in various times and various circumstances, merge into a complex nexus of causes and effects, plural, that create the phenomenon we name global warming.

The simple cause/effect chain occurs locally. I light my cigarette in one place, and throw it out the window in one place. The fire begins in that place and spreads to a region continuous with that place. The event begins as, and remains, local. But in ethopoesis, the cause/effect nexus and the event or phenomenon is global. Though I am currently seated at my computer, drawing electricity, that electricity was produced somewhere else, and the emissions from the production of that electricity are being released not here in my home office, but where the energy was produced. The food that I eat is not itself, here at my dinner table, releasing hydrocarbons, but I purchased it at a grocery store, which got it from a distributor, which procured it from farms in Mexico, so it was shipped over great distance. Hydrocarbons were burned during the shipping, rather than at the moment of my meal, and released across that distance, rather than being released here. The effects of global warming don't follow me around like the little rain cloud in a comic strip; they cloud the entire globe. The strengthened storms and higher temperatures might affect someone on the other side of the planet more directly than they affect me.

For ethotechnical concerns, a rule is adequate. For example, the rule not to leave campfires unattended is adequate, in contrast to the rule not to use fossil fuels. Or, again, the rule don't put your elbows on the table is an adequate rule, in contrast to the rule be a good parent, which needs so much further interpretation and amplification that in an important sense it's no help. It's a good principle in that my children will be happier if I manage to fulfill it, but it's no good at all in the sense that it offers me no guidance. In ethotechne there is an applicable rule that can be enacted; in ethopoesis, there is not. In this regard, the contrast between ethotechne and ethopoesis resembles that in Christian theology between law, which seeks to enumerate the rules that will be adequate to guide me through any and every occasion, and grace, which changes my condition.

The ethotechnical calls for a particular behavior. In relation to forests, I am called upon not to leave campfires unattended, and not to discard cigarette butts that I have not fully extinguished. The ethopoetic calls not for a particular behavior but for an altered, elevated personhood. My particular behavior of raking up leaves manually, rather than using a motorized leaf blower, may be positively inflected, but it is so minuscule as to be invisible, utterly ineffective. In the ethopoetic, my whole person is called into question, and called to involvement. If in ethotechne I am told "You must alter your behavior," in ethopoesis I bear Rilke's charge that "You must revise your life."

In the ethotechnical, there is an interpretation of the given charge that makes my fulfilling that charge possible to me. Not so in the ethopoetic, where no interpretation of the charge would make it possible for me to fulfill it adequately and fully. I have never caused a forest fire, and I never will cause a forest fire. I will never leave a campfire unattended, nor will I ever throw an unextinguished cigarette butt out a car window. But I could not prevent global warming. It's not that I am failing to do something that would prevent global warming, but that nothing I can do would prevent global warming. Global warming ought to be prevented, but no interpretation of that call results in its being possible for me to fulfill the call.

The ethotechnical offers itself in either/or terms. Either I have or I have not left a campfire unattended. Either I have or I have not thrown a cigarette butt out the window. The ethopoetic offers itself as a continuum. I might participate more actively or less actively in the creation of global warming. I might participate more self-consciously or less self-consciously, more reflectively or less reflectively. I might maximize my complicity in global warming, or minimize it. I might, for instance, regularly drive my very large SUV to and from the office or on long cross-country drives, which would increase my complicity, or I might walk to work or ride my bike, or take shared commuter transit, any of which would decrease my complicity.

The ethotechnical offers itself as, or purports to work by, summation. If all visitors to national parks in the United States next year follow Smokey's advice, then the sum of those separate and individual decisions will be that no human-caused forest fires will occur. By contrast, matters of ethopoetic concern operate according to wholeness, a wholeness that exceeds summation. It is plausible to think that this year every human being might decide not to leave campfires unattended; it is not plausible to think that this year all humans will cease to burn fossil fuels. The greater the number of individuals who follow the appropriate rules, the smaller the number of forest fires caused by humans. In contrast, even the decisions by a great many people to stop using hydrocarbons would not stop the process of global warming. I might myself cut my carbon footprint to a tenth of its current size, and I might convince a thousand of my closest Facebook friends to do so also, but global warming would not cease as a result. A larger whole would have to be changed, rather than the sum of many individual parts changing, in order for that to happen.

Ethotechne is a matter of conscience: even insofar as it impacts others, it remains something that I do individually and am responsible for individually. Whether it does or does not affect other people, whether or not other people are aware of it, I am responsible. Even in a circumstance where no one else knows that I set the forest fire, I still am accountable for setting it. Ethopoesis is more like what Socrates resigns himself to in the *Crito*, a life formation inseparable from the larger human community, so that it is not a matter of individual conscience alone. Even though Socrates was condemned for something he didn't do, the condemnation applies. He ought to accept the penalty imposed on him, because it is a part of, or is an effluence of, the whole in which his life has been and is enmeshed. The larger-than-himself, the entirety, is definitive, rather than he himself, the part. Socrates has an individual conscience, but it is not what governs in this matter.

In ethotechnical matters I am called on to obey. The rule not to leave campfires unattended describes something I should simply do. I am duty-bound to obey that principle. I am essentially passive in relation to it, and my obedience occurs, for all practical purposes, in isolation from anything else. The attribute required of me by the ethopoetic is something larger, that, not exhausted by obedience to a rule and not defined by its relation to a nation-state, includes my own judgment in relation to natural constraints, the judgments of others, and so on. I am in active, reciprocal, *responsible* relationship with global warming, a relationship inextricably linked to other aspects of my thought and life.

Louis Mackey's distinction between a problem and a mystery applies here. A problem, he says, "can be solved. The terms in which it is stated define what will count as a solution. Confronted on a math test with a problem that cannot be solved, the student has every right to complain that it 'isn't really a problem.'" A mystery resembles a problem in being "an indeterminate situation that begs to be made determinate," but, unlike a problem, "its indeterminacy is such that the description of the mystery does not specify conditions of resolution and closure." A mystery "cannot be fully described. Faced with a mystery, you can never be sure what will count as a solution, or even that there is one." The ethotechnical offers itself to us in the form of a problem, the ethopoetic in the form of a mystery. As a result, in the ethotechnical there is a solution available, at least potentially or in principle, but the ethopoetic, because it is a mystery, is not offered in terms of problem and solution. Confronted with a problem, I can discover (or *in principle* I can discover, or I *seek* to discover) a solution. How do I keep from causing forest fires?, I ask myself. Oh, I see: I'll thoroughly douse my campfire before I leave my campsite, and carefully stub out each of my cigarette butts. I need only act in a manner adequate to an occasion. Confronted with a mystery, though, I cannot simply find the right switch to flip. No occasion offers itself; I and my conditions must be remade. When I ask how I can keep from causing global warming, I must imagine an alternative self and alternative conditions.

In relation to forest fires I ought to exercise my capacity for what the Greeks called *techne*, but in relation to global warming techne is inadequate, and I ought to draw on my capacity for what they called *poesis*. The techne/poesis distinction in Greek bears some resemblance to the craft/art distinction in English, and indeed "techne" is often translated "craft." The invocation of the capacity for poesis offers at last a succinct way to state the case toward which all along this exploration has aimed. The Greek word *techne* is of course the etymological root of the English word *technology*, and *poesis* the root of *poetry*. The understanding of contemporary life I seek to contest, the one which holds that technology has displaced poetry, takes for granted that everything can be treated as a problem. If that were true, then indeed techne is the appropriate means for addressing our concerns, and it is right that technology, as a useful aid to problem-solving, should displace poetry. If, however, as I contend, the most pressing current concerns of humankind (such as global warming) and the perennial concerns of humankind (such as war) and the most important concerns of human individuals (such as love) are not problems but mysteries, then our greater need is not technology but poetry, and the increased *prominence* of technology in contemporary society is deceptive, masking the continuing greater *importance* of poetry.

1.2: Poetry Against Poems

As commonly conceived, craft orients poetry by and toward *better*, but the counterconception I propose, "metacraft," recognizes also the possibility of orienting poetry by and toward *otherwise*.

I take the former conception as prevalent enough to count as common sense. Asked why she was teaching a workshop on craft, a poet likely would reply that such a workshop would help her students become better poets. Asked why he was taking a workshop on craft, a student likely would reply that he was seeking to write better poetry. Either might add *of course*. It seems obvious, even self-evident. But that common-sense conception of craft takes for granted that writing poetry is a *skill*, acquired by approximating a given standard, and achieved by realizing in poems that standard. To hone my craft is to make my poetry more poetic, to make my poems look more like poems.

That common-sense conception of craft, though, makes poetry inherently conservative, by definition the preservation of structure already in place: to approximate a given standard is to approximate a *given* standard, to reproduce a status quo, reinforce an establishment. Besides, it does not account for all the phenomena. *Paradise Lost*, say, does "look like poetry": presented with an unidentified reproduction of a page from *Paradise Lost*, in a context that created no prior expectation that poetry would be presented, any contemporary reader of English would recognize it immediately as poetry. But presented with, say, page 115 of Claudia Rankine's *Don't Let Me Be Lonely*, which simply lists names of pharmaceutical companies, or with page 45 of Jena Osman's *The Network*, which gives a chart tracing several seemingly unrelated English words back to a common Latin root, or with pages 56 and 57 of Lisa Fishman's *Flower Cart*, which offer a photoreproduction of two pages from a workbook called "Trees I Have Seen," partially filled in with handwriting dated 1910, the same reader of English would be unlikely to identify it as poetry. Without context, the reader might call the Rankine page a list, the Osman a chart, and the Fishman a photocopy, but probably would not call any of the three poetry until offered cues such as surrounding pages from the book, or the book's self-identification as poetry.

By "metacraft," I mean to name and describe a sense of craft that accommodates both Milton *and* Rankine and Osman and Fishman, a sense that recognizes both poetry's capacity to fulfill existing standards *and* to contest those standards. The common-sense conception of craft is realized by making one's poetry look *more* like poetry; metacraft adds the possibility of making one's poetry look *less* like poetry.

In *On Ethics and Economics*, Amartya Sen suggests that "economics has had two rather different origins," one concerned primarily with "ethics" and the other primarily "with what may be called 'engineering.'" The two traditions, he says, focus on different questions. The ethics-related tradition asks about human motivation (posing such questions as "How should one live?") and about social achievement (posing such questions as "What is the good for humans?"). The engineering-related tradition, in contrast, takes its ends as given, and seeks only "to find the appropriate means to serve them." Sen affirms the value of *both* traditions, but in his own work he gives more emphasis to the ethics-related tradition because "the nature of modern economics has been substantially impoverished" by keeping the two traditions separate and focusing almost exclusively on the engineering tradition. There is an analogy to be drawn, in connection with craft in writing. It would be typical to take for granted that in the study and practice of craft, the point is for us as poets to get better at what we do. But that *assumes* that *what we do* is a given, and the only relevant aim is to do that given thing *better* than we are doing it already; and *that* corresponds to what Sen calls the engineering-related tradition. Here I highlight the *additional* possibility, the one corresponding to Sen's ethics-related tradition: in it we might seek to write not *better* than before but *other* than before. In a chess camp or a basketball camp, rather than an MFA program, exclusive attention to the engineering-related tradition might be warranted: there would be no point in considering whether next time, instead of trying to checkmate my opponent's king, I should try to arrange my own pieces into a pretty diamond shape on the board, or in weighing whether, instead of trying to get the ball through the hoop, I ought to see how many cars in a row I could roll the ball under in the parking lot. In chess or in basketball, doing *better* what we were doing really would be the only meaningful possibility.

But writing is not chess or basketball, and in this respect at least, writing is not *like* chess or basketball. In writing, it is legitimate to seek to fulfill received standards, but *also* to ask after the available or possible standards, with the prospect left open that, upon deliberation, I might elect and enact standards that differ from those that previously I took as given. To quote Sen once more, this time from *The Idea of Justice*: "We can not only assess our decisions, given our objectives and values; we can also scrutinize the critical sustainability of these objectives and values themselves."

One might distinguish, then, between two approaches to reflection on poetry. An ethics-related approach would ask about poetry's motivations (posing such questions as "What ought a poem achieve?") and about poetry's effects (posing such questions as "What is a poem about?," meaning both "What is a poem *up to*?" and "What is a poem *speaking of*?"). An engineering-related approach would ask after the techniques and processes that transform "normal" language into "poetic" language, prose into poetry. Those approaches host different questions about craft. The ethics-related approach suggests questioning along the lines of "*What* can I do now, that I could not do before?" The engineering-related approach suggests such questioning as "*How* can I do better what I am doing?" Sen believes that economics has been impoverished by keeping the ethics-related and engineering-related traditions separate and attending almost exclusively to the engineering tradition; analogously, poetry has been impoverished by keeping the two approaches separate and devoting much more attention to the engineering approach. Emphasis on the engineering approach shows itself in the unanimity, the *givenness*, of the sense that the point of an MFA program would be to help us as poets get better at what we do. But *both* approaches have validity. *Both* are necessary.

Another way to get at this point would be to assert that in the *teaching* of craft one ought to push students toward *not* writing better poems. The formulation is willfully perverse, but I *mean* by it that any concept of "better" presupposes an ideal. There may be enterprises for which the ideal is settled, such as chess and basketball, but poetry is *not* one of those enterprises. It's why poetry matters more than basketball or chess: in poetry, the ideal is not *given*, but ever *at stake*. In our critical reception of works of art, we often acknowledge the variability of ideals. If, for example, I were to ask a cinephile which is the better movie, *Taxi Driver* or *Standard Operating Procedure*, she surely would respond, rightly, that the two films are trying to do very different things. You can't say which is better until you specify what you *mean* by "better." But our willingness to describe what we are doing in an MFA as "learning to write better poems" is analogous to asking which movie is better; it is an engineering approach that needs in complement an ethics approach.

If by "craft" we typically denote something analogous to Sen's engineering-related approach (an attempt to internalize, and to replicate in our work, given poetic ideals and techniques), then it seems to me valuable to supplement "craft" with "metacraft" (a self-conscious questioning of ideals and techniques that keeps open, rather than foreclosing, the issue of what poetry *is* and what it might *be* and *do*). Let "metacraft" designate such a poetic practice, one in which ideals and techniques are not given once and for all, but remain ever at stake in the poem and for the poet.

In an essay, Robert Creeley reports having been told once by John Frederick Nims "a lovely story" about another poet's having been asked, after a reading, "that next to last poem you read — was that a real poem or did you just make it up yourself?" The anecdote is funny because it reveals the limitations of (by reducing to absurdity) a certain understanding of what a "real poem" is. The questioner probably conceived of a "real poem" in terms given by what someone with formal education in literature might name "canonicity": a poem, on such an account, is a literary artifact that has been preserved, and has had conferred on it cultural status of a sort that exacts reverence, because it was written by an historical figure long dead, and since deemed by relevant authorities (textbooks, teachers) deserving of the honorific "Poet." Creeley and Nims could share a laugh over the story because their ideas of a "real poem" resembled one another more than either one resembled the idea of a "real poem" held by the questioner in the story. And Creeley can count on our laughing with him, because he can reasonably assume that any reader of his essays will think of a "real poem" in terms more like his own and Nims's than like the questioner's.

But.

If I grant the questioner his conception of a "real poem," then the question stops being a false dilemma: something that "you just made up yourself" in fact *couldn't* be a real poem. Consequently, far from being funny or absurd, it would be perfectly reasonable and appropriate to ask a reader which kind of thing he had just read. Similarly, if I *don't* grant Creeley *his* conception of a "real poem," it becomes clear that Creeley does *have* a conception, one that, no less than the questioner's, has limitations. Creeley's conception, too, picks out certain things as poems, and not others; it affords poetry certain powers but denies it others. Then the rub: once I recognize that Creeley's conception of a "real poem" is *a* conception, not *the* conception, I see that my conception, too, is *a* conception.

This realization suggests that working at my craft might take the form of *refining* my craft (doing even *better* what I am doing), but it also might take the form of *renewing* my craft (doing *differently* what I have been doing). That is, the recognition that my conception of a "real poem" is *a* conception, not *the* conception, invites me to ask (even *obliges* me to ask) what possibilities are opened (and what ones closed) if I adopt another conception. In Sen's terms, it invites me to add an ethics approach to my study and my practice of poetry, not confine myself exclusively to an engineering approach. Recognition that my conception of poetry is *a* conception urges me to complement my attention to and pursuit of *craft* with attention to and pursuit of *metacraft*.

George Lakoff's *Women, Fire, and Dangerous Things* offers a construct that helps toward this aim. Lakoff speaks of "idealized cognitive models" (ICMs), structures by means of which we organize our knowledge. ICMs *function* in a given human context, but do not correspond to preexisting realities. The concept of a "weekend," for example, "requires a notion of a *work week* of five days followed by a break of two days, superimposed on the seven-day calendar," but this reveals that it is idealized, not "real," since "seven-day weeks do not exist objectively in nature." Lakoff further distinguishes "cluster models," in which "a number of cognitive models combine to form a complex cluster that is psychologically more basic than the models taken individually." An example is "mother." One would think that for so important a concept we would be able to "give clear necessary and sufficient conditions" that would "fit all the cases and apply equally to all of them." But in fact no possible definition can "cover the full range of cases," because "mother" employs *various* ICMs, including such divergent models as: the birth model (the mother is "the person who gives birth"); the genetic model (the mother is "the female who contributes the genetic material"); the nurturance model (the mother is "the female adult who nurtures and raises a child"); the marital model (the mother is "the wife of the father"); and the genealogical model (the mother is "the closest female ancestor"). So if, say, I was adopted by one woman, who died soon after, and raised by the woman who raised her, then the birth model identifies one person as my mother, the marital model picks out another, and the nurturance model yet another.

Lakoff goes on to point out that "when the cluster of models that jointly characterize a concept diverge, there is still a strong pull to view one as the most important." The model construed as most important, the "privileged model," often needs qualification, as when we find ourselves needing to describe someone as a "*stepmother, surrogate mother, adoptive mother, foster mother, biological mother,*" etc., which happens when the various models don't converge. Lakoff's point is that "the concept *mother* is not clearly defined, once and for all, in terms of common necessary and sufficient conditions. There need be no necessary and sufficient conditions for motherhood shared by... biological mothers, donor mothers..., surrogate mothers..., adoptive mothers, unwed mothers who give their children up for adoption, and stepmothers." I propose that "poetry," like "mother," is a "cluster model," and that the availability of widely varied privileged models for poetry, combined with the impossibility of giving necessary and sufficient conditions that cover all cases of poetry, makes a practice of metacraft incumbent on all of us who write poetry.

Recognizing poetry as a cluster model, and consequently recognizing the variety of privileged models available, helps explain the Creeley anecdote: Creeley and Nims, one sees, privileged one model, and the questioner privileged another. Recognizing poetry as a cluster model also means that no model of poetry is validated by correspondence with some real and eternal Platonic ideal: to reiterate Lakoff's words, "the concept [*poem*] is not clearly defined, once and for all, in terms of common necessary and sufficient conditions." *No one's* model is right unconditionally or universally. Not Creeley's, not Helen Vendler's or Paul Muldoon's, not yours, not mine. Creeley and Nims can laugh together at the questioner because they privilege the same model, but not because their model is the "right" or "true" model. Recognizing poetry as a "cluster model" reveals that what is at stake in my writing poetry is not only how robustly I realize my privileged model of "a real poem" (i.e. *how* I write), but also *which model I privilege* (i.e. *what* I write).

No cognitive model of poetry is more widely accepted than that based on a contrast between prose, presented "continuously" on the page, and poetry, broken into lines. This "lineation model" shows up in ways as varied as the familiar joke about converting prose into poetry by expanding the margins, and J. V. Cunningham's assertion that "as prose is written in sentences, without significant lineation, so poetry is written in sentences and lines." However common this model may be, though, it is *not* comprehensive. To note one obvious exception, there is by now a long tradition of the "prose poem," whose very name indicates both its claim to be poetry and its refusal to privilege the cognitive model that would make lineation definitive of poetry. History, too, says that the lineation model can't be comprehensive, and was not always privileged. Recall that the *Iliad* and the *Odyssey*, those most canonical of canonical poems, were composed orally, by illiterate singers. *Our* sense of line is orthographic: a line for us is a typographical convention, something that, even if it *represents* something metrical, is *realized as* something fundamentally visual, something that occurs *on the page*, in *writing*. If our sense of lineation were not orthographic, our jokes about composing poetry by expanding the margins would make no sense. But the Homeric singers could not have been thinking in such terms. The "line" for them was aural, not visual, and oral, not written; it was metrical, with no orthographic aspect at all. Homeric singers didn't make a contrast between poetry and prose, so such a contrast couldn't have been the model for Homeric poetry.

That has everything to do with the Claudia Rankine book. *Don't Let Me Be Lonely* is printed as prose, but the book is tagged for marketing purposes ambiguously as "lyric essay / poetry." It couldn't have been written if Rankine had accepted as her model for poetry the contrast between poetry and prose. The page referred to above, the list of pharmaceutical companies, defies the lineation model. Yet lists have value for us, including potential emotional value: the most obvious example of a list laden with emotional value is the Vietnam Veterans Memorial in Washington, D.C., which simply *lists names*. Rankine's list turns out to be a list of the "thirty-nine drug companies [that] filed suit in order to prevent South Africa's manufacture of generic AIDS drugs," a suit that attempts to enforce the companies' claim to own, as "intellectual property," antiretrovirals, thus protecting their own profits, though doing so would entail the deaths of millions of people, the great majority of "the five million South Africans infected by the HIV virus." Rankine laments in the poem that "it is not possible to communicate how useless, how much like a skin-sack of uselessness I felt." The list of pharmaceutical companies comes *close* to communicating that, though. When I face the Vietnam Veterans Memorial, I understand the irrecoverable loss of thousands of lives of individual human persons in a different way than before, with an emotional immediacy that my general awareness of the fact of those deaths does not possess; similarly, when I see Rankine's list of pharmaceutical companies, I understand *her* uselessness because I recognize it as *my own* uselessness in the face of, and my complicity in the fact of, colonialist plunder of material wealth and scorn for human life. I understand my uselessness and complicity in a different way than before, with far greater immediacy. If we do not wish for that possibility to be excluded from poetry, then we cannot accept as given or fixed the lineation model as our way of thinking of poetry.

The lineation model is inadequate, but what about the model Aristotle proposes in the *Poetics*? He specifically states that the lineation model won't do: "the distinction between historian and poet is not in the one writing prose and the other verse." Even in verse, Herodotus still would be history, and the difference between history and poetry "consists really in this, that the one describes the thing that has been, and the other a kind of thing that might be," which makes poetry "more philosophic and of graver import than history, since its statements are of the nature of universals, whereas those of history are singulars." Call this the "algebraic model." If the lineation model establishes parameters for poetry by differentiating it from *prose*, the algebraic model constructs poetry by differentiating it from *history*. History documents the facts, accounting for what actually occurred. Poetry portrays the necessities and principles that underlie the facts, accounting for what did not in fact occur but *might have*, and *may yet*. Poetry's contrast with history resembles algebra's contrast with arithmetic. The arithmetic equation $2 + 2 = 4$ tells me that the two bananas I had today for breakfast and the two I had yesterday total four bananas. The algebraic equation $x + .02x = y$ tells me how much *any* salary would be after a two percent raise. It is hypothetical, in the logical form of material implication: if a particular thing happens in particular conditions, then the result will be such-and-such. It tells me that if I made $100,000 last year and got a two-percent raise, I'd make $102,000 this year; and it tells me that, even though I *didn't* make $100,000 last year, and I didn't get *any* raise.

This "algebraic model" gives a way of finding *King Lear*, a play about events that never happened, and persons who never existed, more edifying than *The Decline and Fall of the Roman Empire*, a history of events that did happen and were performed by persons who did exist. Or again, of finding *The Waste Land*, though Eliot's characters were invented, more edifying than *Democracy in America*, though Tocqueville's characters were "real people." Yet, for all its virtues, the algebraic model cannot be all things to all poems. Where, to name one instance, would the *Divine Comedy*, with its many "real people," even people of Dante's personal acquaintance, fit in this scheme?

Jena Osman could hardly have included in *The Network* the etymology charts of which the page referred to above is an instance, if she accepted Aristotle's model as her own. Osman wants to include in her book, and to *emphasize*, the *factuality* of language. As she herself formulates things on the first page of her book, "Rather than invent a world, I want a different means to understand this one. I follow Cecilia Vicuña's instruction to use an etymological dictionary: 'To enter words in order to see.'" Osman's book enacts a premise formulated in this way by Jan Zwicky: "Few words are capsized on the surface of language, subject to every redefining breeze. Most, though they have drifted, are nonetheless anchored, their meanings holding out for centuries." Words, though they change, do not change *randomly*, so any word contains in itself a form of history, is itself a kind of history. It is this history that Osman seeks to access, and to make available to a reader willing to wonder how Wall Street came to have the power it does over our country and over our lives.

Etymologies are forms of association, to which Osman adds other forms, such as maps and chronologies. Forms of association invite further association, as for example when Osman gives a chronology, listing various events in the order of their occurrence, identifying them by the year of their occurrence, and ending with this event:

> 1920: A horse and buggy loaded with dynamite explodes in front of the J.P. Morgan Bank, killing 40 people. Although the perpetrators are never identified, the event fuels suspicion of immigrants and anarchists and builds support for the deportation of foreigners. **Wall** Street and the financial markets become a patriotic symbol; questioning the economic system becomes anti-American. *The Washington Post* calls the bombing "an act of war... The bomb outrage in New York emphasizes the extent to which the alien scum from the cesspools and sewers of the Old World has polluted the clear spring of American democracy."

Because chains of association ask to be continued, Osman does not have to *tell* her readers to note the points of analogy between this event and the events of 9/11. Simply offering it as the last item in a chronology invites continuation of the chronology with the association to that later event. But the association is between *historical* events. Osman's *poetry* bases itself in, and purports to present, *history*. Aristotle's privileged model of poetry as a contrast to history doesn't cover this case; Osman must have had some other privileged model in mind when she was writing her book.

A third common cognitive model is proposed by Shakespeare's Theseus in the familiar speech from *A Midsummer Night's Dream*, in which "The lunatic, the lover, and the poet / Are of imagination all compact." The lunatic sees devils everywhere, the lover sees beauties everywhere. The frenzied poet sees what isn't there: "as imagination bodies forth / The forms of things unknown, the poet's pen / Turns them to shapes, and gives to aery nothing / A local habitation and a name." The model Theseus offers is exciting enough, bordering as it does on sex and madness. Poetry, his model would have it, is poetry not by contrast with prose, as in the lineation model, or with history, as in the algebraic model, but with *reason*. Call this the "fantastic model." In it, poetry is the discursive result of *seeing things*. The lunatic imagines things that aren't there, but fails to make and maintain a distinction between things that aren't there and things that are. The lover sees *one* thing, the beloved, as he or she is not. The poet experiences the same press of imagination as the lunatic or the lover, but *records* it, displays it to others in words. Poetry records fantasy, the seeing of unreality in place of reality.

Like the lineation model and the algebraic model, the fantastic model, according to which the poet is animated, even overwhelmed, by her hyperactive imagination, enjoys currency in popular culture, but Lisa Fishman could not have written *Flower Cart* if she had accepted it. Fishman opens her book, not with something she *imagined*, but with something she *found*. The first full page of her book contains not a single word she herself wrote: it's a photocopy, reproducing a 1916 letter from F. J. Sievers, the Superintendent of the Milwaukee County School of Agriculture and Domestic Economy, to Mr. C. E. McLenegan of the Public Library in Milwaukee, describing the results of tests performed on a sample of corn sent by McLenegan. Fishman is not transcending "cool reason" by means of her own "shaping fantasies." She is, if anything, *applying* cool reason to a decidedly non-fantastic document. Fishman's poetry does not begin in "aery nothing," but in fully material somethings. About the items reproduced in *Flower Cart*, such as the fieldbook about trees and the 1916 letter about corn, Fishman claims that she did not have "an intention or purpose or 'project' in mind" for them. Instead, she "transcribed and/or materially reproduced [them] after years of living with them and feeling in contact with them in ways not clear to myself," including them in the book as an attempt "to understand why they became necessary to me, how they were functioning, what they have to do, for me, with writing or with the possibility of writing." *Flower Cart* is not imagined by bodying forth "forms of things unknown." Fishman has *found* things, and seeks in her poetry to prevent them from *becoming* unknown.

How I conceive of poetry (what I think poetry *is*) will go a long way toward determining what I can and cannot do in my poems. By keeping "live" the question of how to conceive of poetry, my practice of poetry will have not only the technical aspect we name "craft," which asks "What means will help me achieve my ends?," but also a conceptual aspect I have here named "metacraft," which asks "What ends might I, or ought I, embrace?" As exemplified by the ways Rankine, Osman, and Fishman realize in their poetry possibilities not available to the most common models of poetry, a practice of metacraft (my reconsidering what I think a "real poem" is) might, no less than a practice of craft (increased mastery of anaphora or metonymy, say), create for my poetry possibilities not previously available to me, expanding the range of what I can "just make up myself."

Article 2:
Double stance, double vision.

2.1: Poetry For Relationship

Ambiguity can sometimes make things murky. "Her recommendation letter was ambiguous," I might grouse. "I couldn't tell whether she was praising him or sending us a warning signal." But ambiguity includes, as William Empson observes, "any verbal nuance, however slight, which gives room for alternative reactions to the same piece of language," and sometimes presenting alternatives makes things *clearer*, not murkier. That giving of room for alternative reactions can *clarify* instead of blurring; it can make things *more* specific, not less. The ambiguities in Elizabeth Bishop's poetry perform that clarifying, specifying function well.

It matters that there be such ambiguity. Customarily, we think of our world as a world of *things*. Asked "What is this world made of?," a person might respond by listing things. "Look around you," she might suggest. "Our world is made of chairs and coffee mugs and windows and shirts and trees and people and such." This common-sense view is sanctioned by the grammar of the English language, which stocks our sentences with things: subjects and objects. *The horse galloped across the field*, we might say. The *things* there, the horse and the field, are the "substantives." We say that "galloped" gives information about the horse, but it would sound awkward and odd to say that the horse gives information about "galloped." In English, the horse and the field are the realities. Even that word, "realities," embodies the common-sense notion: "reality" comes from the Latin word *res*, meaning *thing*. What is real has thingness; it is *real* because it is a *thing*.

But what if the common-sense view (that the world is made of things) is misleading? We easily recognize it as misleading in certain contexts. If I'm trying to account for the earth's apparent stability, I'll soon err if I appeal only to things. Atlas is holding up the world, I might postulate. And what about Atlas? Ummm, he's standing on top of... a turtle. And the turtle? For a satisfying account, what we need is not a thing but a force: gravity. We need, that is to say, a *relationship*. "Gravity" does not name a *thing* that occupies the space between the earth and the sun: it names a *relationship* that holds between the earth and the sun. "The world," Wittgenstein reminds us, "is the totality of facts, not of things."

If the world consisted, first and foremost, of things, then in our language uses (our poems, our stories, our essays) we would want always to *dis*ambiguate. We'd want to analyze, to take things apart so we could see each *thing* on its own, separated from the rest, taken *out* of its relationships. We would want our words to pick out one thing at a time, and ambiguity would impede and corrupt our analysis. If, however, our world consists not so much of things as of relationships, then we *want* ambiguity. We *need* it. Only ambiguity, itself a *relationship* between meanings, could hope adequately to signify relationship. We can't say what holds between things if we're too exclusively intent on *separating* things. Ultimately, we're after not analysis but synthesis: not taking things apart but putting them together. We don't want to *eliminate* ambiguity, we want to *get good at it*. And Elizabeth Bishop is *very* good. Her ambiguities are a form of truth-telling, a very rich and apt means toward better understanding ourselves and our world. The various forms of ambiguity in Bishop's work matter, because they enable her poetry to reveal — to *clarify* — a truth about Being (the world, and human experience in the world) that the very grammar of our language works to distort and conceal.

The first form of ambiguity to note in Bishop is *lexical* ambiguity: double entendre, using a word (or words) in a way that enables it (or them) to sustain more than one meaning. One example occurs in Bishop's poem "The Bight," with her use of the word "correspondences." The poem presents itself as little more than a quiet (if quirky) description of the bight at a particular moment, identified by its being at low tide. The speaker simply observes the bight with all her senses. She sees the colors of "the little white boats" and the "[b]lack-and-white man-of-war birds" and the "[w]hite, crumbling ribs of marl"; she hears the "little ocher dredge at work off the end of the dock" as it noisily "plays the dry perfectly off-beat claves"; she smells the water "turning to gas," as if to match its visual resemblance to "the gas flame turned as low as possible"; by identification with the birds, she feels the crash of diving "unnecessarily hard" into the water, and (despite her declaring them "impalpable") the drafts of rising air above it; and indirectly, by extension from "the blue-gray shark tails" that "are hung up to dry" on the "fence of chicken wire along the dock," she tastes the shark-tail soup in a Chinese restaurant. But the poem's very first line alerts us not to think that the water's surface exhausts the bight. "At low tide like this" we can see into the water, under its surface, because it is so sheer, and of course we can see a great deal that at high tide is submerged. The reader is invited to recognize that if there is much going on beneath the surface of the *water*, there may be much going on beneath the surface of the *poem*, too.

Lexical ambiguity creates some of that sub-surface activity. When the poem declares the bight "littered with old correspondences," the word "correspondences" can be taken in at least two ways. Bishop has just introduced the metaphor of letters: the previous line describes piled-up, unsalvaged white boats as resembling "torn-open, unanswered letters," so the most obvious meaning of "correspondences" is letters, as in "I still maintain regular correspondences with two friends from school." The bight at low tide, strewn with all those boats on their sides, resembles, Bishop suggests, a desktop strewn with letters. But "correspondences" also designates ways in which things resemble or reflect one another, as in "There are many correspondences between poetry and film." Both meanings are "live" in the poem, and the double entendre is not just a gimmick, a flaunting of verbal dexterity. It inflects the rest of the poem: the fact that this *word* has two meanings entails that the whole *poem* does, also. In one, the unsalvaged boats alone are the correspondences: they litter the bight as unanswered letters litter a desktop. We could specify this meaning by rewriting Bishop's sentence to read, "Some of the little white boats are still piled up... like torn-open, unanswered letters. / The bight is littered with *these* old correspondences." On this reading, we are told what the correspondences are. On another reading, though, the boats are *representative* correspondences. They themselves are correspondences, but they also suggest the presence of *additional* correspondences. We could specify this meaning by rewriting Bishop's sentence to read, "Some of the little white boats are still piled up... like torn-open, unanswered letters. / The bight is littered with old correspondences *like these*." On this reading, we are told that the correspondences are numerous, but not told what they are. We must discern for ourselves what items participate in correspondences, and what they correspond *with* or correspond *to*. The poem is closed (in telling us what to think) *and* open (in leaving us to decide for ourselves what to think).

The lexical ambiguity in "correspondences" hints at additional lexical ambiguity at work in this poem, as for example the pun in that same line. "The bight is littered with old correspondences" sounds very like "The bight is literate with old correspondences." That light-handed homophonic resonance adds to the poem's presentation of the bight as a place full of information and story, to be *read*. Or, again, in the last line the words "awful" and "cheerful" have a subtle duplicity to them. They seem to impute qualities to the activity itself: the activity is awful, and the activity is also cheerful. Since the poem has been talking about things, not about people, it is natural to extend the awe and cheer to those things. What is the awful and cheerful activity filling with awe and cheer? The dredge that is performing the activity. But the states that correspond to those qualities, awe and cheer, are *human* states. Humans experience awe and cheer, but dredges and sponge boats do not. So the more plausible extension is to the nearest human. Who is the awful and cheerful activity filling with awe and cheer? The speaker. This ambiguity, the dissonance between the more natural extension and the more plausible one (or, to put it differently, the location of the awe and cheer in the dredge *and* in me), establishes a *relationship* between the human observer and the things observed. It litters the poem with *correspondences*.

Bishop creates ambiguities with her words, certainly, but with her sentences as well. A beautiful example of her syntactical ambiguity occurs in "Filling Station." The poem gives a bemused description of a very dirty filling station, so "oil-soaked, oil-permeated" that it elicits from the speaker the warning, "Be careful with that match!" The family members who staff the station all are dirty, the wickerwork furniture on the station's porch is dirty, the doily atop the wicker taboret is dirty, the potted plant beside it is dirty. Yet, the speaker marvels, that all-pervading oiliness notwithstanding, somebody embroidered the doily, somebody waters the plant, and somebody "arranges the rows of cans / so that they softly say: / ESSO—SO—SO—SO / to high-strung automobiles." The last line, with its summation of the speaker's surprise, contains a clarifying ambiguity. "Somebody loves us all" might mean that each of us has at least one somebody who loves us, though the somebody who loves me is not the *same* somebody as the somebody who loves you; or it might mean that there is one somebody, the *same* somebody for everyone, who loves each of us. Those two meanings are *very* different. The first is a social and existential reassurance; the second, a spiritual and metaphysical reassurance. They cast themselves back over the poem very differently, giving the whole poem a double meaning. The first meaning, that each of us is loved by our own somebody, takes the filling station as evidence that we humans can and do offer one another consolation no matter how otherwise uncaring and unkempt our circumstances. I may be poor and shabby, but somebody loves me nevertheless. You may drive a more high-strung automobile than I do, but so what? I've got just as much love as you. The second meaning, that we all of us are loved by the same somebody, makes the filling station into an instance (however humble) of the argument from design, which contends that the whole world and everything in it, we ourselves included, has its origin and fulfilment in, and is suffused with, care.

That ambiguity enables "Filling Station" to portray as complementary, or even equivalent, two forms of understanding and hope that typically are construed as diametrically opposed. The poem embodies as equal possibilities and equal presences two very different integrities, just as the Nekker cube and the duck-rabbit do:

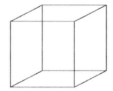 

Is the right-hand square the closer face of the cube? Yes. Is it the farther? Yes. Is the figure a duck? Yes. Is it a rabbit? Yes. Both integrities remain "live." In "Filling Station," reading the ambiguous last sentence in one way foregrounds in the whole poem one presence; reading it the other way foregrounds the other. In the reading in which there are as many somebodies who love us as there are us who are loved, our human love is the consolation we can and do give one another in the face of the world's entropy and ugliness. All is "quite thoroughly dirty." Against this ultimate dirtiness, we ourselves can, and others in fact do, embroider doilies, water plants, and arrange rows of cans into symmetrical order. Love is a form of resistance to, or mitigation of, or compensation for, the world's "disturbing, over-all / black translucency." In the reading in which there is one some-body who does the loving, the same Somebody in every case, the situa-tion is reversed. The embroidering and arranging are not done against the ultimate dirtiness; they *are* ultimate. The dirtiness is mere appearance, underneath which they are the reality. Love does not contest an ultimate disorder; it manifests an ultimate order. Love is not something we do for one another to contest the world, but instead is what the world itself does for us. We are used to thinking of these as mutually exclusive possibilities: if we must console ourselves for the dirty world's indifference, then the world can't care for us and arrange things on our behalf. Yet in the poem both worldviews are equally present, just as the duck and the rabbit are equally present in the one figure.

Yet a third kind of ambiguity in Bishop's poetry, temporal ambiguity, is an important element of "The Fish," in which the speaker catches "a tremendous fish," but ultimately decides to "let the fish go." Everything in the poem happens in past tense: I caught a fish, I held him up, I looked at him, and so on. In the last line, though, *let* is conjugated differently from the other verbs in the poem. "Caught," for example, is only the past tense of "catch," not also the present tense; "held" is only the past tense of "hold," not also the present tense; and so on. "Let," though, is not only the past tense of "let," as in "Yesterday at lunch I let Susie cut in line." As that past tense form, "let" describes a one-time event. But "let" is also the perpetual present tense, as in "When my little brother and I play ping-pong, I let him win." As this perpetual present tense form, "let" describes a recurring or continuing event. Context typically chooses one tense for us. If I say, "I let my roommate have the best parking space," I might mean I did it once, or I might mean I do it always. Context chooses. If I say, "We had a fight yesterday before he left for work, so when he got home I let my roommate have the best parking space," I mean to describe a one-time event that occurred in the past and has been completed. If I say, "His parole officer says it's best not to upset him, so I let my roommate have the best parking space," I mean to describe a recurring event, still going on, not yet com-plete. In Bishop's poem, though, the context does not enforce a choice, but allows either reading: at the past moment I have been describing, I allowed the fish to go, or as an ongoing condition I continue to allow the fish to go.

As a result of this ambiguity, I occupy two different relationships to the release of the fish: I did it once, on that day I am recalling from the past, *and* I am always releasing the fish. The event happened once, and the event is always happening. To reiterate why all of this matters: if "let" were *not* ambiguous, if it were only the past tense form, it would refer to an event and a thing, the release of the fish. Because it is ambiguous, because it is also the perpetual present tense form, it designates also a *relationship* between a self I was in the past and the self I am now.

It confirms the recognition that Bishop does not restrict herself to one form of ambiguity per poem, that the temporal ambiguity of the line is complemented by syntactical ambiguity. "I let the fish go" can mean "I let go of the fish" or "I allowed the fish to go." In one case I perform the action, and in the other I authorize the action. In one the fish got his way, in the other I got my way. Thus is the relationship between myself and the fish made more nuanced.

Bishop's "First Death in Nova Scotia" exemplifies a perspectival ambiguity: it offers the point of view of a child experiencing a funeral, limited to her child's understanding, *and* the point of view of an adult looking back with an adult's understanding on the child's experience. An adult speaker recalls an event from her childhood, the funeral of her infant cousin Arthur. On the one hand, the descriptions all are calculated to place us in the child's head, so that we look out on this domestic interior through the child's eyes. As the reader, I see the stuffed loon as the child sees it, and from the position of the child. I experience being lifted up, so that I see the coffin from below at first, and then from above after I have been lifted up. And so on. Yet at the same time I see the whole space and the whole experience from the point of view of the adult narrator, looking onto the scene through *her* eyes. I look *at* the child being lifted up, I look at the child looking at the coffin, and so on. Duck and rabbit both are present in one figure, and similarly the child's point of view and the adult's point of view both are present in this poem.

Like the other forms of ambiguity, perspectival ambiguity *matters*: it is a condition for morality. If I cannot imagine myself in the way Bishop imagines herself in this poem, as *both* an interested agent *and* an impartial spectator, then I cannot assess the moral worth of a decision or action. Neither perspective by itself is enough. If I can see myself only as an agent,

I can act only out of greed. If I can see myself only as a spectator, I cannot act at all. Only the dynamic tension of both perspectives together, the *relationship* between my agent and spectator selves, enables me to think and act morally.

The particular perspectival ambiguity in this poem, the simultaneous presence of a child's point of view and an adult's, may resonate especially strongly for readers steeped from childhood, as Bishop herself was, in the language of Christianity. It might call to mind, for instance, these words attributed to Jesus in the Gospel of Matthew: "Verily I say unto you, Except ye be converted, and become as little children, ye shall not enter into the kingdom of heaven. Whosoever therefore shall humble himself as this little child, the same is the greatest in the kingdom of heaven." Or, again, these words of Paul: "When I was a child, I spake as a child, I understood as a child, I thought as a child: but when I became a man, I put away childish things." Whatever credence one does or does not accord those texts from that particular religious tradition, and whatever interpretation one puts upon them, they at least involve some form of interaction, some dynamic tension, between the perspective of a child and the perspective of an adult, and they advise some form of attention to both perspectives.

In "One Art," the speaker declares that "the art of losing isn't hard to master," a proposition she expands on by enumerating things one might lose (door keys, places, names, intentions...), and by then enumerating things she herself has lost. The list of losses, possible and actual, culminates in "you (the joking voice, a gesture / I love)." "One Art" compactly and perfectly illustrates all the forms of ambiguity identified so far. Lexical ambiguity is at work in the word "master," which can mean "get good at" or "overcome." This gives two very different readings to the first line and its variants. "The art of losing isn't hard to get good at" establishes one aim, but "the art of losing isn't hard to overcome" establishes an opposite aim. In the former reading, I am trying to do more and better losing; in the latter, I am trying to stop losing. Syntactical ambiguity occurs in the penultimate line, itself one of those variants of the first line. The line might be read to mean, "the art of losing is not so difficult that it cannot be overcome," or "it is not difficult to get good at the art of losing." In the one case, what is not too hard is the art of losing, and in the other what is not too hard is the mastering of it. Temporal ambiguity, too, is present in the last stanza. Has the losing of you already occurred, or is it inevitably going to occur? I lost my mother's watch, and I lost two cities, so the first reading of "Even losing you" would be that it has happened already, in the past. But then the next verb tense is in the future: "I shan't have lied..." That makes "Even losing you" read as "Even when I have lost you" (i.e. even in the future when I lose you), I will not have lied. As in the last line of "The Fish," this temporal ambiguity establishes a relationship between a self I was and a self I am or might be. Finally, there is perspectival ambiguity in the use of the second person: in the third stanza, the "you" in "where it was you meant / to travel" seems to be the reader. But in the last stanza, the "you" in "Even losing you" is the beloved. So, as in "First Death in Nova Scotia," I the reader am given both points of view, that of the beloved and that of the neutral bystander.

To those forms of ambiguity, "One Art" adds tonal ambiguity, which arises from its use of a form of understatement I'll call "parastatement," familiar from its presence, for instance, in such canonical works as Shakespeare's sonnet 130, with its declaration that "My mistress' eyes are nothing like the sun; / Coral is far more red than her lips' red; / If snow be white, why then her breasts are dun; / If hairs be wires, black wires grow on her head." This string of insults lists ways in which the beloved fails to live up to the standards of feminine beauty prevalent then and there: her eyes are dim; her lips are not red; her breasts are not white; her hair is like wires; her cheeks are not rosy; and she has bad breath. But we know that this is a form of praise whether or not we ourselves embrace those standards of beauty, and even before the "And yet" that signals the speaker's making the praise explicit by declaring, "I think my love as rare / As any she belied with false compare."

Shakespeare's poem inverts the familiar rhetorical device we call "faint praise." If I ask a friend what she thinks of my latest book and she says, "The cover is beautifully designed," she will have *communicated* clearly something she didn't *say*. The same parastatement at work in "high culture" also functions in popular culture, as in Lucinda Williams' country song "Jackson": "All the way to Jackson / I don't think I'll miss you much"; "Once I get to Baton Rouge / I won't cry a tear for you"; and so on. We know the speaker *means* something other than what she *says*. She *is* going to miss her ex all the way to Jackson; she *is* going to cry when she gets to

Baton Rouge. In "One Art," too, we know that the losses the speaker repeatedly insists are *not* disasters really *are* disasters, *especially* the "losing you" that the speaker introduces, with true parastatement, as "even losing you."

Parastatement is understatement in the form of protesting too much. I call it tonal ambiguity because each aspect carries with it a tone: the Shakespeare sonnet has a tone of dismissal and one of admiration; the Lucinda Williams song has a tone of resolve and one of despair; and "One Art" has a tone of flippant unconcern and one of inconsolable grief. Parastatement plays on a first-order/second-order distinction, of the sort Lynne McFall makes in distinguishing second-order from first-order volitions. A second-order volition, she says, "is a complex desire: a second-order desire to have a certain first-order desire be one's will: to be the desire that moves one to action." McFall illustrates the distinction with smoking: "I want to want not to smoke, and I want this desire, rather than the desire to smoke, to be the one that is effective." The dissonance between the first- and second-order desires enables me to make one desire present by stating the other. Stating the second-order desire ("I wish I didn't want a cigarette right now") expresses forcefully, without actually stating it, the first-order desire: I want a cigarette right now. That same dissonance is at work in "One Art." The second-order desire, I wish I wouldn't get upset over losing things I love, is the one that gets stated, but the first-order desire, I wish I hadn't lost so many things I love, is *more* forcefully expressed *because* it is not stated.

Parastatement proves particularly useful for circumventing censorship. It is a way of saying the unsayable. Bishop, with her privileged economic background and powerful connections, may seem an unlikely victim of censorship, but her personal life bears on this poem. The "I" and the "you" in the poem are very open, and we as readers may fill in the poem's "you" with whom we will. "One Art" reads beautifully and effectively if I know nothing about Elizabeth Bishop, and read myself as the "I" and my long-lost one true love as the "you," regardless of my gender or that of my beloved. But in Bishop's time the social pressure directed against homosexuality was so active and pervasive that her loves could not be named in her poems, nor her love affairs described explicitly. At least two of those loves, though, seem clearly to be among the losses lamented in "One Art."

Bishop lived in Brazil for more than a decade with the architect Lota de Macedo Soares; in 1967 Soares committed suicide by overdosing on tranquilizers. They lived in Petrópolis, at the convergence of the Quitandinha and Piabanha rivers. Even if Lota cannot be named in the poem, "two rivers" and "a continent" make her present in it. And the "you" addressed in the last stanza is apparently Alice Methfessel, a much younger woman whom Bishop met when she returned to Boston after her years in Brazil. "One Art" was written during a period when Methfessel was engaged, apparently soon to be lost to Bishop. Societally-imposed sanction forbade Bishop direct expression of grief over her same-sex beloveds, so Bishop chose a way to *express* that grief without *stating* it.

One additional ambiguity makes the last line of "One Art" an appropriate culmination to this inquiry. "*Write* it!" has a homophone, "*Right* it!" We write disasters when and because we cannot right them. We may extend to others of Bishop's poems what might be said of "One Art," and to others' poems what might be said of Bishop's: disasters she could not right, she wrote.

2.2: Poetry For Justice

In its robust use of a craft technique I'll call "critical third," Gwendolyn Brooks's "The Lovers of the Poor" demonstrates that craft decisions are not merely *decorative*, not ex post facto flourishes tacked onto the surface of a structure that precedes them, but that, to the contrary, craft decisions determine the structure, influence the function, and participate in the political orientation of the work. Through craft decisions we shape our ideas and emotions, enhance our best understandings, and enact our ideals.

Adrienne Rich recommends reflection not only on the *means* of writing but also on its *ends*, "not how to write poetry, but wherefore." Brooks's "The Lovers of the Poor" depicts one way in which that *how* and *wherefore* join, a way in which *craft* decisions have ethical/political valence. It offers a case in point to second Audre Lorde's declaration that poetry is a "vital necessity" because of these two truths: that "the quality of light by which we scrutinize our lives has direct bearing upon the product which we live, and upon the changes which we hope to bring about through those lives," and that the craft decisions we make in our work influence "the quality of the light within which we predicate our hopes and dreams toward survival and change, first made into language, then into idea, then into more tangible action." Brooks's poem shows one way in which a poem can change "the quality of light by which we scrutinize our lives."

From what we see in popular culture (and from what some of us were taught in school), it would be easy to arrive at the notion that poetry is good only for registering intense private emotions: it's a fit vehicle for declarations of love or outpourings of grief, but for little else. "The Lovers of the Poor," though, offers one counterexample to such constriction. "The Lovers of the Poor" reminds us that, in addition to its capacity to record "emotion recollected in tranquility," poetry can also depict and critique injustice, speak to matters of social welfare and public policy, and so on. It reminds us that even our seemingly most private emotions occur in, and are shaped by, a broader context. It gives one answer to the question "How can poetry serve the interest of social justice at least as robustly as it answers the impulse toward self-expression?" In 1960, the year "The Lovers of the Poor" was published in book form, even though she had won the Pulitzer Prize ten years before, Gwendolyn Brooks, had she lived in, say, Memphis, could not have married a white person or shared a meal at a restaurant with a white person or even drunk from the same water fountain as a white person. Where she did live, Chicago, her society did not allow her to make even mundane life choices without attention to pressing civic concerns such as racial inequalities; it would be most surprising if she wrote poetry that did not attend to such concerns. But *how* does it attend to such concerns? Critical third is one of its means.

In "The Lovers of the Poor," the point of view appears at first to be an instance of "close third," or what, in *How Fiction Works*, James Wood calls "free indirect style." In close third, the narrator moves fluidly between looking *at* a character from outside and reporting that character's thoughts and feelings from inside: the narrator can report things that the character could not know (just as an omniscient narrator would be able to), and also report the character's internal state with full acquaintance (just as a first-person narrator would).

Imputing to close third much power, Wood offers an account of *why* it is so effective. According to Wood, in close third "the narrative seems to float away from the novelist and take on the properties of the character." Wood makes up brief examples to contrast direct speech with indirect, and thus to show what makes "free indirect speech" free and indirect. Direct speech: "He looked over at his wife. 'She looks so unhappy,' he thought, 'almost sick.' He wondered what to say." Indirect speech: "He looked at his wife. Yes, she was tiresomely unhappy again, almost sick. What the hell should he say?" In direct speech, quotation marks and other cues clearly differentiate the author's perspective from the character's. In indirect speech, the cues are removed, so the perspectives of author and character merge rather than remaining distinct. In the first case, the judgment that the character's wife is unhappy is attributed clearly and exclusively to the character; in the second case, that judgment might have been made either by the character or by the author, or by both. The benefit of close third, on Wood's view, is that readers see things through the character's eyes and language *and* through those of the author. "We inhabit omniscience and partiality at once," he says. Between author and character yawns a gap, and close third "simultaneously closes that gap and draws attention to it," which makes close third a form of dramatic irony, a way "to see through a character's eyes while being encouraged to see more than the character can see."

The point of view in "The Lovers of the Poor," though, seems to me to demonstrate a difference from close third as Wood describes it, a difference significant enough that the point of view in Brooks's poem merits a new name: not "close third" but "critical third." The advantage of *close* third, on Wood's view, is that we "inhabit omniscience and partiality at once." The advantage of *critical* third, I contend, is not that we inhabit at once partiality and *omniscience* but that we inhabit at once partiality and *impartiality*. If in close third the authorial perspective resembles that of God, in critical third the authorial perspective resembles that of an impartial spectator.

The impartial spectator is an imaginative construct introduced by Adam Smith, to explain how we come to regulate our passions and motives by ethical criteria rather than exclusively on the basis of perceived self-interest. Smith alleges that our sentiments "have always some secret reference either to what are, or to what upon a certain condition would be, or to what we imagine ought to be the sentiments of others. We examine [our conduct] as we imagine an impartial spectator would examine it." Having entered into "all the passions and motives which influenced" that conduct, we either "approve of it by sympathy with the approbation of this supposed equitable judge" or else "we enter into his disapprobation and condemn it." Smith considers the ability to imagine and enter into the perspective of the impartial spectator a *necessary* condition for moral self-awareness. His idea is simple: as long as I stay conceptually within my own subject position, only my self-interest participates in my judgment, so my decisions have prudential, but not ethical, character. Only by imaginatively occupying a hypothetical subject position, and judging as such a subject would judge, can I make ethical decisions. I become capable of equitable judgment only when I can see *what* an equitable judge would see, and *as* an equitable judge would see. Just as I can see myself only with the aid of a device such as a mirror or camera, so, according to Smith, I can think ethically only with the aid of a device, the impartial spectator.

Smith's position inflects ethical judgment with a literary character: it is conditioned by, and inseparable from, an act of narrative imagination. In "The Lovers of the Poor," Brooks applies Smith's insight, inflecting her *poem* with ethical character. Critical third manifests the reciprocity between the ethical and the literary. In the course of depicting characters *failing* to imagine themselves into the impartial spectator's position, Brooks makes that impartial spectator's position available to the reader. In point of view, she does in her poem what Smith says we must do in order to think ethically. To the tension that Wood says close third creates ("Can we reconcile the author's perceptions and language with the character's perceptions and language?"), *close* third can respond only in aesthetic terms. The tension can become too great, as according to Wood it does in John Updike's novel *Terrorist*, in which the main character, a schoolboy, sounds less like, say, Holden Caulfield, than like, well, John Updike. When the tension in close third becomes too great, the result, Wood says, is a failure of *style*. But in answer to that same question, "Can we reconcile the author's perceptions and language with the character's perceptions and language?," *critical* third responds in *ethical* terms. Brooks's poem demonstrates that critical third succeeds or fails in ethical and political terms no less than in aesthetic terms.

The shift from omniscience (in close third) to impartiality (in critical third) is momentous. As a writer, I occupy the position of God: I make all things happen. I *can* be omniscient: I know what the protagonist in my novel is thinking at any moment, because *I* decide what that protagonist is thinking. As a reader, though, I occupy a limited, human position: my participation does not at all resemble God's, but instead happens under severe constraints. I *cannot* be omniscient: if the writer hasn't *told* me what the protagonist is (either directly or indirectly) thinking, then I don't *know* what the protagonist is thinking. Wood's close third, then, in inhabiting partiality and omniscience at once, imposes an unbridgeable gap between author and reader: the reader can look at but not share in the author's omniscience. But because critical third inhabits partiality and impartiality at once, it *unites* author and reader: *both* can imagine themselves into impartiality.

Anyone who has watched team sports has seen players on the sideline near the end of a close game praying for victory, committing a theological error that is relevant here: they want God to keep and employ all his Godly powers, including omnipotence and omniscience, but they want God to put those godly powers into action *without impartiality*. They think God is a fan of *their* team. They've met the conditions for close third: partiality and omniscience are present at once. They haven't met the conditions, though, for critical third: they won't allow impartiality to temper their partiality. The praying players don't recognize the perspective of their opponents, and the ladies in Brooks's poem don't recognize the perspective of the poor. But *that* is what critical third does, and it is why Brooks employs critical third in this poem. The ladies from the Ladies' Betterment League, like the praying players, do not allow impartiality to temper their partiality, but Brooks, by showing us the ladies' flight from impartiality, makes that impartiality present in the poem, available to us as readers.

"The Lovers of the Poor" offers a straightforward narrative. Two wealthy, middle-aged white women, representatives of a charitable organization called "The Ladies' Betterment League," pay a visit to a rundown apartment building in a slum, with the intention of giving money to relieve the poverty of a black woman who lives there, toward what they consider her "betterment." The two visitors observe conditions that they did not expect to encounter, such as newspapers used as rugs, and rats on the prowl. Horrified by those conditions, and unable to reconcile them with their preconceptions about the people they understand themselves to be "bettering," the ladies quickly retreat, hastening to return to the more opulent conditions in which they themselves live.

Critical third operates throughout the poem. Is it the ladies themselves who notice the afternoon sunlight "slanting / In diluted gold bars across the boulevard," or is it the author who sees the sunlight in just that way? Two people would be unlikely to arrive independently at such a description, but it could have been made by either author or character with equal likelihood. Some of the phrasing early in the poem could "belong" to either author or character, and even when a locution clearly belongs to one agent's perspective, we do not stay there long. Describing the ladies' love as "barbarously fair" seems like a judgment made by the author, not likely to be shared with the ladies themselves, but immediately after that authorial declaration we move to the teachings of the ladies' mothers, reported in words that "present" as if they are from the mothers' own mouths: "You'd better not be cruel! / You had better not throw stones upon the wrens!" Recall that all these elements of the poem were craft *decisions*. Brooks could have called the poem "A Visit," and begun the first line "The lovers of the poor arrive," but she *chose* to call the poem "The Lovers of the Poor," and to begin with the indented and no-initial-capital "arrive." Brooks could have written, "Whose mothers taught them never to be cruel, / And never to throw stones at little songbirds," but she *chose* to report the mothers' counsel in words that might be from the mothers' own mouths. Brooks didn't *happen onto* critical third by accident: she made *decisions* (word by word, line by line, sentence by sentence) that established that point of view in the poem.

The alternation between perspectives continues throughout the poem. For example, the description of the ladies as "full, / Sleek, tender-clad, fit, fiftyish, a-glow" seems clearly authorial, not the way a self-consciously polite person would describe herself. But then in the next stanza, the description of the poor as "The worthy poor. The very very worthy / And beautiful poor" seems exaggeratedly aligned with the characters of the ladies, as if the author were out-ladying the ladies, reducing to absurdity their preconception. In direct speech, the beginning of the third stanza might go something like this: "'But it's all so bad!,' they told themselves. 'It's entirely too much for us.'" Brooks, though, has the line read "But it's all so bad! and entirely too much for them." As with Wood's example of close third, in this example of critical third the judgment is not attributed exclusively to the characters in question, but might be the characters' judgment, or the author's, or it might be a judgment shared by characters and author. This line opens a thirty-line segment detailing what is bad and too much for the ladies, the whole segment exemplifying the author/character double perspective at work in critical third. For example, on the one hand, the list of items that contribute to the stench includes "and, they're told, / Something called chitterlings," which seems clearly an authorial *report* on the ladies' perspective, an authorial declaration that the ladies don't know what chitterlings are and don't recognize the aroma of chitterlings being cooked. On the other hand, though, the lamentation that the slum is "Not Lake Forest, Glencoe. / Nothing is sturdy, nothing is majestic," might be the ladies' own words, from their own perspective.

The impartial perspective receives formulation in other ways as well. For instance, the poor live in a world to which only common nouns apply: urine, beans, diapers, soil, rugs, children, quilts. The ladies, though, live in a world replete with proper nouns: Spode, Lowestoft, Chippendale, Aubussons, Palm Beach, Art Institute, Michigan. The ladies get brand names, the poor get knock-offs and generic. This distinction, not *announced* by the authorial voice, is applied consistently. "The Lovers of the Poor" does not "preach," yet it performs a powerful political critique, not by declaring and arguing for a political platform or thesis, but by *showing* the outcome of fulfilling other assumptions. It shows the ladies refusing to look impartially at themselves or others, and by their refusal transforming themselves into beasts: they leave "at what they manage of a canter." At the end of the poem they return to their prior partiality by "resuming all the clues of what they were" and keeping themselves from "inhaling the laden air." By showing the ladies' flight from impartiality, Brooks makes that impartiality present along with the ladies' partiality in the poem.

Martha Nussbaum argues that imagining the impartial spectator, which she takes literature as furthering, is crucial for agents in our judicial system. The impartial spectator has "the power of imagining vividly what it is like to be each of the persons whose situations he imagines"; consequently, "compassion and sympathy, but also fear, grief, anger, hope, and certain types of love are felt by the spectator as a result of his vivid imagining." Appropriate emotions offer "recognitions of the character of the situation before us"; the impartial spectator fosters such emotion, thus "leading us in a pleasing natural way into the attitude that befits a good citizen and judge." The impartial spectator, and the reader of literature, according to Nussbaum, "learns an emotional repertory that is rich and intense but free from the special bias that derives from knowing one's own personal stake in the outcome." The benefits that Nussbaum identifies as attending the point of view of the impartial spectator attend Brooks's poem, where that point of view is present.

Amartya Sen lists four advantages of the impartial spectator over social contract theory as a basis for justice: the impartial spectator can assess comparatively without need for a transcendental solution to issues of justice; the impartial spectator can take note "of social realizations and not only the demands of institutions and rules"; the impartial spectator can provide guidance toward social justice even without completeness in social assessment; and the impartial spectator can take note "of voices beyond the membership of the contractarian group, either to take note of their interests, or to avoid our being trapped in local parochialism." Through its attainment of impartiality by means of what I am calling critical third, "The Lovers of the Poor" realizes all four of the advantages that Sen expects from the impartial spectator. It is able to make a comparative assessment of the situations of the ladies and the poor, and comparative assessment of the actual situation of the poor with the situation the ladies imagine for the poor, without needing first to have a global solution to inequitable distribution of wealth in capitalist economies or to the long history of racial injustice in the U.S. It is able to look at the actual results of the ladies' attempted beneficence, not only the institutions (such as the Ladies' Betterment League) that create the event in the poem or the rules (do not "throw stones upon the wrens") that the ladies take themselves to be following. The poem can guide us toward social justice without need for a totalizing theory of poverty and racial prejudice. And, perhaps most importantly, it can take note of the interests of the poor in the poem, though they are only nominally but not in actual effect members of the contractarian group, and can offer a way out of the parochialism in which the ladies are trapped.

Brooks's application of critical third testifies that poetry's capacities are not limited to "private," prudential concerns; poetry can also address "public" matters such as issues of social justice. Brooks's poem does not focus primarily on the strategies the popular conception of poetry's capacities might lead one to expect: its appeal is not primarily emotional but critical; it does not achieve its effect primarily by creating *sympathy* with the citizeness but by drawing the ladies into question; it does not present a vision that foregrounds charity but one that foregrounds justice. Poetry need not choose between avoiding political matters and being "preachy": it can elevate "the quality of light by which we scrutinize our lives."

Article 3:
Think making, make thinking.

3.1: Poetry Against Philosophy

Suppose I stop by one day to borrow your burro. "I need your ass," I say to you. "No can do," you reply. "I had to put Don down. But how about Howard, my horse?" "Thanks, but no," I say. "My donkey Hettie is in heat. I wanted Don for stud, to continue Hettie's line. A sterile mule for offspring wouldn't do." In such a case, the answer to "do donkeys and horses correlate?" is no. They would bring different results, one well-suited to the purpose at hand, one not. But change the situation slightly. This time, I've dropped in to borrow Don for a backcountry pack trip with my brother-in-law. My brother-in-law is an ass most of the time, and Howard is a sturdy horse: here Howard in Don's stead will do just fine. Do donkeys and horses correlate? This time, yes.

Then how about the acts of language we name "poetry" and "philosophy": do *they* correlate? Plato famously said "no." Philosophy should rule, he demanded, and poetry suffer exile. Most typically, Plato's answer has been taken as imposing an adequacy condition on any "yes" answer: for my answer "yes, they *do* correlate" to stand, it must imply that Plato's "no, they don't" is wrong. The yes and the no are mutually exclusive: any rationale that would float my yes must first sink Plato's no. But can that adequacy condition be presupposed? The donkey/horse thought experiment says it does not hold. Here at least, one "no" does not necessarily preclude another "yes." Insofar as recognizing something's identity consists in simultaneous acts of collocation and isolation, insofar as it consists, in other words, of definition by genus and species, its results will vary not only by *what* is compared, but also by *why*, toward what end, the comparison is made.

Poets have reason to answer yes to the question of whether poetry and philosophy can correlate. Louis Mackey gives grounds for doing so. A philosopher who does not accept Plato's "no" as setting conditions for any future "yes," Mackey gives *philosophical* grounds for correlating poetry and philosophy, a way of watching them discipline one another on terms other than Plato's clumsy false dilemma. Mackey's ways of troubling distinctions between philosophy and poetry offer guideposts for poets and philosophers alike.

One alias by which nowadays it goes, this saying-yes of poets to the correlation of poetry and philosophy, is "poetics," which I use here in two senses: broadly, to refer to all inquiry into the nature, meaning, and value of poetry; and narrowly, to name that inquiry as practiced today by a cluster of poets and critics who claim the term "poetics" for their explorations. Contemporary poetics often blurs the distinction between poetry and philosophy, appropriating for poetry some of the qualities or aims often assigned to philosophy. Here are four examples of poetics in the act of appropriating the philosophical, chosen if not at random then primarily for their concision. Leslie Scalapino contends that "Poetry in this time and nation is doing the work of philosophy — it is writing that is conjecture." Charles Bernstein argues "that a number of poets working in English today are mounting a sustained critique of the norms of description and argument and that this critique has important implications for the forms not only of poetic discourse but also for the forms of critical and philosophical discourse." Specifically, "active questioning" in poetics "of the relation of form and style to content" implies "that there can be no neutral form of philosophical or critical argument." Gerald L. Bruns asserts "that poetry is philosophically interesting when it is innovative not just in its practices but, before everything else, in its poetics (that is, in its concepts or theories of itself). Poetry is as much a conceptual art," he says, "as it is an art of language." Finally, Lyn Hejinian claims the language of poetry as "a language of inquiry, not the language of a genre."

A whole range of contemporary modes of inquiry — philosophy, literary criticism, linguistics, sociology, and so on — recognize the role opposition plays in constructing meaning, a recognition from which they know not to take for granted the pairing of terms into facile contrasts (black/white, good/evil, and so on). Poetics, too, is attuned in this way, and I take the four short passages just quoted to suggest that, whatever other oppositions it suspects, poetics mistrusts any opposition of poetry to philosophy that would make them mutually exclusive. Louis Mackey does from a starting point within philosophy what those writers on poetics do from a starting point within poetry.

Though he taught in a university philosophy department, Mackey recognized from the beginning of his career that his investigations would have implications for poetics. The preface to *A Kind of Poet* (published in 1971) recognizes illumination of poetics as a crucial element of the book's value. "I am persuaded that the study of Kierkegaard can throw a new light on the meaning of poetry and — in view of his conjunction of 'poet and thinker' — on the relationships between poetry and philosophy." Mackey's work casts new light on the meaning of poetry not only through the study of Kierkegaard but also through Sorrentino or Scotus, Derrida or Dick: those authors serve Mackey's preoccupations as the pseudonyms served Kierkegaard's.

Probably most individuals willing to pay any attention at all to poetics would grant it intrinsic value, but Mackey also offers justification for the enterprise to minds more skeptical of it (such as those of most contemporary philosophers). Whether or not poetics has intrinsic worth, Mackey points out, it has instrumental value. To be wrong about the relationship between philosophy and poetry would be to practice philosophy badly, and to be wrong about the world. "Modern philosophers," Mackey says, have "thought it possible to be objective; that is, they have claimed to occupy an existentially neutral standpoint, to view reality from the perspective of the angels." But Mackey follows Kierkegaard in countering that "every standpoint is in fact not neutral but biased, not objective but subjective, not angelic but human and finite." Whatever else it may do or not do, poetics serves as a corrective for philosophy, helping philosophy keep from mistaking its desires (for objectivity, universality, and so on) for actualities. Philosophy may do well to maintain those fictions as regulative ideals, but poetics helps remind philosophy that those fictions *are* fictions.

Beyond helping justify poetics, Mackey also helps refine its practice. As part of its investigation, poetics asks what poetry *does*. Mackey postulates some possible answers, among them that poetry heightens human awareness. Mackey identifies Kierkegaard's explicit purpose ("'*without authority*, to call *attention*...', or 'to make aware'") as "the purpose of every poet: not to tell the truth, nor yet to insinuate fabulous lies, but to make men aware of the options so that the emergence of truth within the individual is not hindered by the conceit of knowledge or the tangle of error." Poetry helps a person attend with enriched awareness to her experience, her culture, the world. It helps liberate its readers or auditors from the "tangle of error" to which people are prone prior to philosophy, and from the "conceit of knowledge" to which philosophy makes us more susceptible.

Another answer to what poetry does occurs when Mackey reads the *Philosophical Fragments* as a performative. What he attributes to that particular poetic utterance might be attributed to poetry more generally. I quote Mackey, replacing at each appearance the book's title with the word "poetry." "[Poetry] is obsessed with alterity. In particular with the question, how can language give expression to that which is wholly other than language?" In response to that question, Mackey says, "Since the other than language cannot be uttered, the text of [poetry] turns back upon itself and becomes an exploration of the limits of language. But since the limit of language is itself the alterity language cannot express, [poetry] neither says nor shows but rather performs the 'absolute paradox': that the limit of language, its irreducible other, is also its radical source." Poetry does not only *recognize* the "absolute paradox" but *realizes* it. In contrast to philosophy, which represses paradox, and thus inevitably brings about the result precisely opposite the aim it pursues (and believes itself to be attaining), namely self-deception and falsehood rather than truth, poetry by embracing the paradox in which language is immersed works *with* the language rather than *against* it.

Just as poetics asks what poetry *does*, it also asks what poetry *is*. Mackey construes poetry as "the aesthetic manifestation of the ironic diremption of essence and phenomenon," by which he means to valorize poetry's approach to essence and phenomenon over philosophy's. Philosophy treats essence and phenomenon as at least in principle reconcilable: each of its various means (critique, phenomenology, symbolic logic, ordinary language, analysis) purports to move us toward unity of essence and phenomenon. Claims to such unity provide the basis for methodological justifications: *we analytical types are better philosophers than those continental types because we tell it like it is*. Poetry, Mackey tells us (with requisite irony), tells it like we tell it, realizing and exploring ironically that its own "substance" — language — simultaneously separates essence from phenomenon and creates the wish for their reunion.

These two inquiries, into what poetry *does* and what poetry *is*, bear directly on one another, as is clear when one considers the role of paradox. Unlike philosophy, or at least unlike contemporary philosophy as Mackey sees it most often being practiced, poetry recognizes its subject as paradoxical, even as paradox. "The beyond-the-text" at which linguistic acts aim (name it what capitalized term you will, God, Truth, Experience) "cannot be comprehended or even adumbrated in the text without becoming itself textual," Mackey says. "In that sense, there is nothing outside the text. And yet it is this 'nonexistent' *hors-texte* that all texts are 'about.'" Because it recognizes the ultimacy of paradox, poetry's aim is "not understanding but ineluctable confrontation." It's not that God is a limit concept, our linguistic approach to which must be apophatic and our existential engagement with whom must be mediated, but that language is a comprehensive vehicle from which no escape (and therefore *only* mediation, nothing like "understanding") is possible. At best, we achieve "confrontation," and that metaphorically, a "facing" language that occurs always and only within language, a realization of the duplicity, not the univocity, of language, which expressed as a term denoting a human subjective stance is irony.

In addition to asking what poetry does and what poetry is, Mackey asks *how* poetry is, one part of an answer to which is that poetry is polyvalent. Hobbes argues that "The *Light* of humane minds is Perspicuous Words, but by exact definitions first snuffed, and purged from ambiguity"; Descartes, that in propositions clarity and distinctness stand in opposition to dreamlikeness. Mackey recognizes the bankruptcy of the Hobbesian/Cartesian ideal, and understands "Kierkegaard's rejection of the modern tradition" as "rooted in his recognition of the poverty of univocity," his response to which was to refuse "the demand for univocity," a refusal which turned philosophy into poetry. Modern philosophy tries to believe it does or even *can* live in the world, which it thinks is essentially unified. Poetry "thinks" it lives in language, the "essence" of which is not to have essence, which would be self-identity, but to be always double and recombinative.

An understanding of what poetry *is* will likely be advanced by identifying what poetry is *like* and clarifying what it is not; by defining it, in other words, by genus and species. Part of the trick here, Mackey points out, is that poetry is like philosophy (it belongs to the same genus, language, and is driven by the same desire), but it is not philosophy. It is like philosophy because "the nostalgia for truth and reality is... as potent as the consciousness of their loss is ineluctable." That likeness, the participation of philosophy and poetry in the same genus, should not deceive us, though, into *identifying* philosophy and poetry. Instead of arguing "that philosophy is only (or is really) poetry," or supposing "poetry to be philosophy," he treats poetry and philosophy as correlatives, in an attempt to "blur all such distinctions, compromise all such discriminations, and thereby evacuate all facile identifications." His point, he says, is "that categories like 'philosophy' and 'poetry' are essentially metastable," and that thus "'philosophy' (as the custodian of necessary truth) and 'poetry' (as the superintendent of possibility and/or the purveyor of lying fables) are not baskets into which all verbal objects may be dropped, but the terms of an uncertain and restless dialectic." It would be a philosophical but not a poetic gesture to try to identify (to make unified and self-identical) philosophy and poetry. That would presume the validity of the philosophical longing for closure, unity, and essence. Mackey prefers the irony of poetry.

Philosophy and poetry do share some standards, on Mackey's view. For example, when he asserts that "the rigor proper to philosophy is its fidelity to the mystery of being by which it is first aroused, to the guardianship of which it is perpetually committed," one implication of which is "that all philosophical problems are formulated and discussed within a context that cannot be saturated or bounded, a context that demands to be articulated in problems, creates problems, but is never exhausted by or reduced to the problems it generates," he follows immediately with the observation that poetry shares that standard. Poetry, too, pursues fidelity to the mystery that occasions it, and poetry can no more exhaust that mystery than philosophy can.

There is a history to the correlation of philosophy and poetry. Like all categories, those two are constructs, and Mackey tells a history in which the categories "poetry" and "philosophy" arose simultaneously and are interdependent. The "founding gesture of philosophy" was an urge "to replace myth altogether with logic, and narrative with discursive modes of exposition." To enact that replacement, philosophy undertakes a "dialectical critique of myth for the sake of truth," as a result of which "truth itself is defined in and by the terms of that critique." Constructing itself as a category by distinguishing itself from myth, philosophy also and by the same gesture creates the category poetry, "the anarchic domain where ignorance and error run riot," undisciplined by truth, which, remember, was not a category for myth, "because the distinction of true and false is first opened up by the dialectical critique of myth and expressible only in discursive form."

Various vexing questions about poetics are raised, directly or indirectly, in Mackey's writings. For instance, early in *A Kind of Poet*, the impossibility of realizing the figure of the poet is broached. "The poet, who represents man's attempt to live his immediacy, is like immediacy itself eternally presupposed but never present." That direct questioning of the possibility of a poet's existing is matched later in the book by an indirect questioning of whether poetry itself is possible. By attending to the question posed on the title page of *Philosophical Fragments*, namely whether it is possible to base an eternal happiness on historical knowledge, which Mackey says is "in effect... the question, Is Christianity true?," Mackey implicitly raises for poetics the question whether the paradoxical heart of poetry is susceptible to the resolution that could count as realization.

Mackey points out that "Kierkegaard was convinced that the questions — What does it mean to exist? What does it mean to believe? — were so ordered that the latter could not be discussed until the sense of the former had been clarified. It is after all a [person] who *believes*." The question of what it means to be a human bears on the question of what it means to have faith. When Mackey later notes the indeterminacy of discourse, we can make a corollary observation on behalf of poetics. What we are as humans conditions what we are as language users. So when Mackey contends that "we think in order to recover the reality forfeit by thinking," when he proposes that to be human is always already to have suffered a broken bond with being, "and the project of thought is to reappropriate in language the being of which language is the alienation," he also implies an ideal for poetry. If "truth and reality are never more than the imagined terms of the nostalgia for a truth and reality never possessed," then "the greater art is the art that embraces this paradox."

One conclusion at which Mackey arrives, and one I here adopt as a consolation of this my (non)philosophy, is the impossibility of conclusion. The work of poetics (like the work of philosophy) is not, and never can be, finished, in part because the movement between them can never be stopped. "Neither the claims of the understanding nor those of the imagination may be forfeit, though it is not possible to define... the terms of their cohabitation." Philosophy insists on the law of excluded middle, and can exist only if everything is either true or false. Poetry is neither true nor false, so as a counterexample to the law of excluded middle that would disprove the law of excluded middle but only by application of the law of excluded middle, it becomes "the self-deconstructing moment in the logic of truth." Philosophy calls it true to choose a side. Mackey prefers poetry's jouissance in seeing each side as and through the other, origin symmetrical, world without end, amen.

3.2: Poetry Against Fragmentation

Philosophers call it a "category mistake" to treat something as if it belonged in a category to which in fact it does not belong, and philosophers consistently make two category mistakes in regard to that influential ancient Greek public intellectual Herakleitos.

One mistake is to pretend that Herakleitos wrote fragments. It is true that nothing of Herakleitos' work has come down to us in continuous or complete form. We might have only a small handful of Sophocles' apparently numerous plays, but what plays we do have are complete; what dialogues we have of Plato might be (ironically) copies of copies, but they are complete. Of Herakleitos, though, we have only very short citations embedded in various works by later authors. Prior translations, without exception, preserve (even emphasize) that fragmentation: *of course* it would be irresponsible to present what has arrived to us as if it had arrived whole. No self-respecting translator would downplay the incompleteness and discontinuity of what we have from Herakleitos.

Yet one of the short passages that has reached us warns, "Let us not thoughtlessly consent to common sense in momentous matters." In this matter at least, the warning is apt: the common sense of things in regard to Herakleitos' work is mistaken. The work has *reached us* in fragments, but Herakleitos didn't *write* in fragments. Of the passages we have, to take their current fragmentation as definitive of their character is to mistake transmission history for original textual architecture. Kirk and Raven fall into this trap, perfectly exemplifying consent to common sense. "The surviving fragments," they opine, "have very much the appearance of oral pronouncements put into a concise and striking, and therefore easily memorable, form; they do not resemble extracts from a continuous written work." Kirk and Raven admit that the one longish passage that appears to have been the opening of Herakleitos' book ("Logos *is* ever...") is "a structurally complicated sentence," plenty continuous to stand as a counterexample to their view, but they wave it away by speculating that "possibly when Heraclitus achieved fame as a sage a collection of his most famous utterances was made, for which a special prologue was composed." With a vicious circularity, Kirk and Raven take this speculation as both supportive of and supported by the view that "the fragments we possess" (as if the "Logos *is* ever..." passage were not one of them) are "obviously framed as oral apothegms rather than as parts of a discursive treatise." Parity of reasoning would sanction a view that the Roman colosseum, because it is now in ruins, must have been originally designed and built as ruins, must in its nature *be* ruins, and that the large intact portion, so unlike the rest, was a later addition.

Even translators alert to the dubiousness of taking current fragmentation as a fulfillment of original form still do not avoid replicating that gesture. Charles H. Kahn, for example, wisely disputes Diels' curious decision to list the surviving passages "in alphabetical order according to the name of the author citing them," and replaces Diels' alphabetical ordering with a thematic ordering, on the premise that "Heraclitus' discourse as a whole was as carefully and artistically composed as are the preserved parts, and that the formal ordering of the whole was as much an element in its total meaning as in the case of any lyric poem from the same period." Yet, that imputation of wholeness notwithstanding, Kahn's book declares itself an edition of "the fragments," and the passages are presented so as to emphasize and enforce their separateness.

In my translation and arrangement of Herakleitos ("Fire at Night," in *Rain Inscription*), I have sought to contest this pattern of exaggerating fragmentation, by grouping the passages and leaving them unnumbered. By minimizing separation between passages, I aim to give greater emphasis to continuity than to division, and by inventing sections, I posit a different *kind* of division than the transmission history has imposed. I neither delude myself into thinking, nor seek to deceive others into believing, that such presentation brings us any *closer to* Herakleitos' original, only that it turns *away from* a particular distortion that until now has been consistently imposed on the surviving passages. Neither the grouping of passages nor the leaving them unnumbered removes distortion. Both strategies do, though, distort *differently* from the usual distortion, a reminder that the usual distortion goes unnoticed only because it is usual, not because it is not distortion. By grouping the passages and leaving them unnumbered, I underline the aspect Kirk and Raven cross out: the continuity and structural complication of the fragments. Prior translators have acted by analogy with a museum curator who presents the shards of an ancient ceramic bowl *as shards*; my translation adopts an alternative strategy, analogous to the curatorial strategy of presenting ceramic shards restored to the shape of a bowl and joined with a neutral binding medium. The curator may not know that the arrangement matches that of the intact bowl, before it was broken, and cannot replace the parts of the bowl that have gone missing, but she *can* present the bowl *as a bowl* rather than *as shards*.

The other category mistake is to treat Herakleitos as a presocratic philosopher. The category "presocratic philosopher" is anachronistic, tendentious, and stultifying. Herakleitos, of course, could hardly have considered himself a "presocratic," and to categorize him in that way is to beg the question, to foreclose the possibility of reading the work on anything approaching its own terms. Categorizing Herakleitos as a presocratic cages the work, guaranteeing that the reader will not "get it." A caged tiger resembles a caged giraffe more closely than it resembles a wild tiger, and a Herakleitos categorized as a presocratic philosopher resembles Thales and Parmenides more than he resembles Herakleitos allowed to stand by himself.

The category "presocratic" is convenient in packaging a history of philosophy, because it sanctions a tidy narrative. A small group of Greeks, the story goes, several of them from Miletus, more or less suddenly broke through the previously unmitigated intellectual confinement of a sensibility centered on Homer, and began to pose in anti-mythical, proto-rational ways a question of origin and essence: What is the *arche*, the original and universal and ultimate substance? Collectively, they ran through various options. Thales proposed that everything is (derives from and consists of) water. Anaximander proposed that everything is composed of *apeiron*, the unbounded. Anaximenes said everything was air, Herakleitos that everything was fire, and so on.

That narrative blurs important distinctions (e.g. for Thales water is what *persists through* change; for Herakleitos fire is what *enforces* change), but its convenience has helped it to persevere quite tenaciously. As with their embrace of fragmentation, so too in this consent to category Kirk and Raven make good whipping boys, having bought into the story without resistance. They recognize that the story is oversimplified: they note that much of our information about the presocratics comes from Theophrastus, who "was strongly influenced by Aristotle," who in turn cared little for "historical objectivity." Kirk and Raven criticize Theophrastus on the grounds that, "once having extracted a general pattern of explanations," he imposed it too boldly, "in cases where he lacked full evidence." Then, having criticized Theophrastus' error, they replicate it, settling (on the very next page) on the general pattern that the presocratics replace mythological gobbledygook with "truly rational attempts to explain the world." The standard view of Thales, Anaximander, Empedocles, Parmenides, et al. groups them together and creates them "the presocratic philosophers" by taking for granted two contrasts: they are philosophers because they differ from their predecessors and contemporaries by introducing rationality into an otherwise irrational (read: poetic, mythological) world-view, and they are presocratics because they differ from Socrates/Plato as children differ from adults, Plato having brought to robust, steady maturity their slender, stumbling, immature first attempts at rationality.

But neither contrast holds for Herakleitos. He explicitly *identifies* his utterance with a poetic and mythological precedent, the Delphic oracle, noting with apparent admiration that it "neither explains nor obfuscates, just signals." Herakleitos does not reject a poetic, mythological mode in favor of a "rational" mode that resembles the pattern of argumentation that contemporary Anglo-American philosophy finds reassuring: he *embraces* a poetic, mythological mode that might be called "oracular," and that does not match, but instead challenges, our standard prototypes of poetry and of philosophy. Its closest alliance is with tragedy, which Édouard Glissant characterizes as "an art of unveiling, not of proposition or analysis."

In her "Oracularity," Jan Zwicky treats oracular utterance as "a kind of figurative pointing, a form of expression that aims to get us to see a conceptual gestalt," but does so "by fingering a contour rather than by providing a full-frontal photograph." To comprehend oracular utterance "involves grasping — even if only dimly and inarticulately — what is being pointed at and that it is being pointed at." Herakleitos does not presage critique or anticipate analysis or foretell elenchus. He is no proto-rationalist, convinced that his discursive protocol will win him mastery over come what may (as, for example, that paradigmatic rationalist, Descartes, convinces himself that his method wins us such mastery that "there can be nothing so remote that we cannot reach to it, nor so recondite that we cannot discover it"). To the contrary, Herakleitos' oracular discursive mode defers, in form and content, to an order greater than himself, inexorable and not at all subject to human mastery, demanding of us first- and second-order observation, provoking us to an interminable search for meaning.

Neither does the second contrast (immature presocratics, mature Plato) hold. Oracles are "the closest analogues in classical culture for Heraclitus' pronouncements," according to James Warren, not only because Herakleitos himself claims them as analogues but also because they are, like Herakleitos' own work, framed as "deliberately ambiguous pronouncements that demand careful attention by the reader to the potentially multiple meanings. A casual interpretation can lead to disastrous results." It is not that Herakleitos' naïve and childish oracular work hints us toward Socrates' sophisticated and grown-up maieutic method (and Plato's dialogical account of it), but that Herakleitean oracularity is itself a fully-realized discursive approach, every bit as high-stakes as Plato's dialogues, and with just as much integrity as they have.

This category mistake I pushed back at by lineation. Imposing line breaks may seem a strange or even arbitrary strategy, but if, as Karla Kelsey contends, line breaks "require the reader to consider the relation of part to whole, the connection between line and sentence and stanza," then imposing line breaks, though it does not restore a *feature* of the original does restore a *quality* of the original. Herakleitos' work exemplifies at least two of the characteristics that Niklas Luhmann attributes to art generally. Luhmann finds art provocative: "What is at stake in art is not a problem to be solved once and for all but a provocation — the provocation of a search for meaning that is constrained by the work of art without necessarily being determined in its results." He also understands art to invite a particular stance that he calls "second-order observation." If the "first-order observer concentrates on what he observes, experiences, and acts out within a horizon of relatively sparse information" and therefore "lives in a world that seems both probable and true," the second-order observer "notices the improbability of first-order observation" because she observes not only what first-order observers observe but also "*how* others observe." Lineation constrains but does not determine, and invites (by tacitly but insistently posing the part/whole question) second-order observation. Lineation may not be the strategy Herakleitos himself used to achieve these ends, but it helps what we now have of Herakleitos achieve them, as what there once was of Herakleitos evidently did. As with the grouping of passages and leaving them unnumbered, imposing lineation is not *not* a distortion, but it is a *different* distortion than the usual distortions, a way of noticing distortions taken so for granted that they go unnoticed.

My translation seeks to recognize Herakleitos' strangeness, and thus keep alive his challenge. Even to the ancients, Herakleitos was known as *ho skoteinos*, the dark one. (The names of the dark northern lands of Scotland and Nova Scotia both derive from *skotos*, the Greek word for darkness.) The metaphor of darkness was applied to Herakleitos not because his work was unclear but because it demands revised perspective. Herakleitos is dark, not because his information is recondite or because his doctrines are difficult to grasp, not because his arguments are intricate and extensive, but because his work when we approach it demands of us a waking-up that is neither easy to achieve nor comfortable to maintain.

Of the physical realm, we learned long ago that force rather than stuff holds us. The earth does not rest on a turtle's back; it is not held up by Atlas. It is "held in place" (it has the movement it has, and the relationship with other bodies) by gravity. In physics, it is implausible to posit a fundament, yet fundamentalism persists in regard to the metaphysical. Many today still insist on equivalents to the turtle: the Ten Commandments, the Qur'an, the Constitution, and so on. Herakleitos, though, keeps the physical and metaphysical realms commensurate. For Herakleitos, it is not by *stasis* but by *dynamis* that what is is as it is and does as it does.

This supervenience of dynamis over stasis, Herakleitos asserts, drives metaphysical and physical alike. In the ethical, it manifests as reciprocity; in the political, as checks and balances; in the discursive, as dialogue; and so on. It also informs Herakleitos' writing, which activates such traits as parataxis and such structures as parallelism in order to reverberate with force rather than resolving into fundamentals. Such grammatical structures epitomize a wholeness, not fragmentation. By attending to them, and by the strategies of grouping, *not* numbering, and lineation, it is possible to recognize Herakleitos as an author not of fragments but of wholes one might call, by coinage from the cognates metaphor and aphorism, *meta-*

phorisms, to see Herakleitos not as one among the several similars who compose the set "the presocratics," but as a unique, a singular thinker and writer whose work remains as vital and challenging today as when it first was written.

Article 4:
See what is at stake, change what is at stake.

4.1: Poetry For Reparation

Ecopoetics faces a basic difficulty: the self-destructiveness of the current relationship between humanity and the rest of terrestrial nature obliges individual humans to *do something*, not to passively accept, and in so doing advance, such practices as, for example, large-scale alteration of rainforest into grazing land or dependence of the cultivation and distribution of food on (finite and non-renewable) petroleum. Yet ecopoetics is a *discursive* practice. What can we *do*, we who *say*? It doesn't *ease* the difficulty, exactly, but does turn toward it instead of away, to remind ourselves that a saying is itself a doing, one that may influence future doings, and to distinguish between two kinds of activism, one of which poetry may support, the other of which poetry may practice. Even without attempting to do justice to the scope of W. S. Merwin's 1998 volume *The Folding Cliffs*, which is more than 300 pages long, one might read it as illustrating, in its presentation of an ideology alternative to the one responsible for the historical event it narrates, the distinction about activism.

Though the stakes for *us* in regard to Merwin's poem are conceptual, social, and ecological, the stakes for *the characters* are physical: disease threatens, or is perceived by them to threaten, the characters' lives and well-being, and the characters threaten one another. European settlers have created and begun to enforce a policy of quarantine for Hawaiians with leprosy, and Ko'olau, who has contracted the disease, decides to resist enforced separation by fleeing, with his wife Pi'ilani and their son, to a part of the island of Kaua'i not yet occupied by the Europeans. The Europeans organize a posse to capture or kill the fleeing couple. Ko'olau and Pi'ilani find a hiding place, where they wait "on a ledge under a deep overhang with big rocks / out in front and between these they could see the valley." Eventually, though, they are discovered, and Ko'olau defends their position.

Once a shot is fired, the conflict becomes a gunfight. Even then, Ko'olau seeks to minimize the conflict and keep his actions defensive, but his antagonist Stolz persists in threat, which forces Ko'olau to complete his defense by killing Stolz: "Paoa called out to him / — He is going to shoot —

and Pi'ilani saw Stolz / on one knee and the gleam of his rifle and Ko'olau fired." His having killed a European solidifies Ko'olau's status as a fugitive from (the Europeans' vision of) justice. His fugitive status continues even after his death: the book opens and closes not by emphasizing the *violence* of the conflict (by portraying the gunfighting) but by emphasizing the *pervasiveness* and *perdurance* of the conflict (by showing Pi'ilani keeping, at the beginning of the book, Ko'olau's gravesite and, at the end, the details of their life secret from the still-threatening Europeans).

Physical conflict enacts ideological conflict. The ideology may be at a low level of abstraction, as in an armed robbery, where one person asserts that the law entitles her to a wallet with a few credit cards in it and another person asserts that need entitles him to that same wallet, or at a high level, as when one nation asserts that God mandates one mode of government and another asserts that Allah mandates a different mode. Any instance, though, puts principles and worldviews, not only cash or occupation, at stake. Any narrative puts ideology at stake for the reader, whatever else may be also at stake for the characters.

Between the physical and ideological conflict in a narrative stands "aesthetic distance." The reader (and the writer, who is also a reader of the written) is an *observer* of the physical conflict in the narrative, but a *participant* in the ideological conflict. That is, I am not caught in the cross-fire when two characters in a story shoot at one another. No reader ever needed emergency surgery for a bullet wound from a character's gun. But I *am* caught in the ideological crossfire. I have views, views on which I base decisions and stake my identity, about who has a right to what wallet, about the relation between providence and the actions of human governments, and about the respective rights of colonizers and colonized.

In regard to the physical conflict of *The Folding Cliffs*, then, I need only concern myself with the characters: I need not worry about my health and safety, or W. S. Merwin's. But in regard to the ideological conflict, I must consider not only the ideologies of the characters, but also the ideology of the author, and my own ideology. The *actions* of the plot are contained within the story, and have to do with me only insofar as I enter the imaginary world of the story, but the ideologies behind those actions spill over into life, and interrogate my ideology. That the plot of *The Folding Cliffs* culminates in a gunfight has no bearing on whether W. S. Merwin in fact owned a gun when he wrote the poem, or whether I own a gun when I read the poem. But the principles and worldviews that motivate the characters' use of guns *do* bear on my views about gun use, and on W. S. Merwin's. The story can change the facts (whether I own a gun, whether I shoot other humans) only by influencing ideology (changing my beliefs about the value of guns and the value of human lives).

Compare three ideological frameworks: that of the protagonists, that of the antagonists, and that of the narrator. Though the terms serve only for convenience and cannot be "pushed" far or "leaned on" heavily, for all the reasons that (for instance) Laura Ann Stoler articulates in *Duress*, call the ideological framework of the protagonists "precolonial," that of the antagonists "colonial," and that of the narrator "postcolonial." The narrative invites, and the narrator expects, us, the readers, to adopt the postcolonial ideological framework. I mean by these frameworks something like this. In regard to the environment, a precolonial framework assumes that humans may be, and ought to be, integrated into the natural environment. Animism and personification of nature suggest that we humans flourish when we submit to the will of, and by that means integrate ourselves within, the natural environment in which we live. A colonial framework assumes that humans ought to (seek to) be masters of the environment. We are different from and superior to nature, which can be made to fulfill our desires and needs. We flourish not when we are integrated within nature, according to its conditions, but when we have mastered it, bent it to our wills. A postcolonial framework sees humans as *necessarily* integrated into the environment, and therefore subject to it in the sense that we cannot separate ourselves from it and stand over against it. The metaphor for integration is not subjection of one party (humans) to the will of the other (nature), but communion, the recognition of common cause and the maintenance of community between the two parties.

A precolonial framework sees the other as something into which to be incorporated, a point of view that explains why indigenous cultures have so often welcomed the strangers who have ultimately conquered and/or assimilated them. For colonials, the other is to be mastered, incorporated into oneself through occupation, elimination, enslavement, or other means. A postcolonial framework sees the other as worthy of respect and understanding, with entitlements and rights analogous to one's own, and with parity between the two, rather than incorporation of one into the other, as the aim. A precolonial framework treats nature as sacred and the other as god; a colonial framework treats nature as "natural resources" available for human use, and the other as a beast to be tamed and used, as one uses cows and chickens; and a postcolonial framework treats nature as that from and within which we evolved, and to whose laws we are subject, and treats the other as an equal of oneself.

In a precolonial framework, "our" point of view is propitiatory: "we" look "up." We look *at* the supernatural, the point of view from which authority and causation enter nature. A colonial framework presumes the lordly point of view in which we are the children of God, made in God's image, so "our" point of view is lordly: "we" look "down." We look *from* the supernatural, and impose authority and causation on nature. (If a single ideological reason had to be adduced, beyond material reasons such as better weaponry, to explain why European settlers consistently conquered indigenous peoples, this would be it: in a meeting between a group with a precolonial framework and a group with a colonial framework, the precolonial group would assume that the others were supernatural, and that they themselves, the precolonials, were subject to them, the colonials. Colonials would assume that the others were natural, and hence subject to the colonials' control.) A postcolonial framework, instead of looking "up" or "down," looks "around," presuming equal validity to narratives and equal participation in authority and causation.

In a precolonial view my well-being will depend on placation, my deferring to god's view. God must be brought to my side. In a colonial view my well-being will demand action, my realizing god's view in the world. God is already on my side. A postcolonial view will construe aligning my view with god's to mean attainment of the hypothetical condition of viewing things *sub specie aeternitatis*, which will be possible to me insofar as I am able to enter into and identify with more than one point of view, and then sum those points of view, through a kind of binocular vision, into a more inclusive point of view, not unlike Srivinas Aravamudan's double view of the "tropicopolitan" as "the colonized subject who exists both as fictive construct of colonial tropology *and* actual resident of tropical space, object of representation *and* agent of resistance." Just such an object of representation and agent of resistance is Merwin's Koʻolau.

The Folding Cliffs elicits a "postcolonial" view. In its narrative the precolonial view is physically defeated by the colonial view, and the colonial view is morally defeated by the precolonial view, leaving, as the alternative with which a reader will identify, the postcolonial ideal of humans respectful toward and integrated with the other: the human other, the natural other, the sacred other.

The physical defeat of the precolonial view by the colonial view occurs on both the communal and the individual level. At the communal level, to cite only one example, "two brothers from New England named Winship" arranged between rival chiefs Kamehameha and Kaumuali'i "enough peace for their own purposes / which involved cornering the traffic in sandalwood," for the harvest of which men were made to work in oppressive conditions, with little to eat and "nothing to wear on the mountain / nothing to cover them when they lay down after dark / on the ground in the cold," leaving them susceptible to illness and starvation. The physical defeat was registered thus on the body politic *as* bodies, but also on the body politic as its relationship to the land. In contrast to the placement on and connection to the land that is grounded in birthplace and working the land, the Europeans installed an economic system that allowed foreign ownership and absentee oversight. In legal terms, that historical occurrence receives succinct summary by Wendie Ellen Schneider: "In the 1840s, under pressure from foreign governments and with the guidance of his missionary advisors," Schneider reports, "Kamehameha III (1824-1854) instituted a sweeping legal transformation in Hawai'i. His reign encompassed a number of radical changes in Hawaiian law, including the introduction of constitutional government and fee simple land tenure."

In addition to thus visiting the community itself, physical defeat visited the individuals *in* the community, through disease, starvation, displacement, and violence. The displacement represents a transitional step from community to individual, in its creation of isolation. Ko'olau and Pi'ilani leave their village as part of a group, but eventually Ko'olau and Pi'ilani and their child must be completely on their own. The displacement occurs quickly. After the group decides to leave, they begin to pack, but are forced to hurry when "they heard / the hollow boom of the howitzer" being fired at them. They pause to look back, just long enough to see their homes being burned by the Europeans, and to see their flight enforced by a group beginning to pursue them: "there was the sound of water back under the overhang / a cool breath from the cliff as they waited until the first / soldiers emerged from the trees below and started toward the cliff."

Nothing in the poem better exemplifies this physical defeat than the death through disease of Ko'olau. The leprosy that forces Ko'olau to flee progresses throughout the flight, eventually becoming gruesome. On his feet "the torn sores were deeper and they never stopped bleeding / and rotten water came out of them" so that "when he walked he left prints of blood and fluid and rags / of flesh trailed behind his footsteps." Finally the disease wins, and Pi'ilani, who "stayed with him until the end" then buried him and "left him there in the sleep of the seasons."

The Hawaiians lose physically, but win morally. The Hawaiians, not the Europeans, maintain courage and solidarity in the face of disease: "Ko'olau noticed that it was the foreigners / whom the sickness almost never attacked who feared it most / and what the Hawaiians dreaded most was being taken / away from their families." That dread even becomes the name of the disease, which Ko'olau calls "the sickness that separates people." The poem depicts the main characters as retaining their pride and autonomy, despite the physical threats and limitations imposed on them. For example, they are shown deciding to die in their own way, a deliberation that ends with Ko'olau resolving that "If it seems / that there is no other way I will try to kill us all / quickly and we will not see the rest," after which resolution "they pulled the child / to them and sat with their arms around each other."

A postcolonial perspective is realized not only negatively, as the contrast between the physical defeat of the precolonial view and the moral defeat of the colonial view, but positively in depictions of the primacy of nature itself and the possibility of human integration with nature. Nature transcends colonial attempts to master it, and provides for those modest enough to seek integration with it rather than mastery over it. Ko'olau, the narrator says, "made his way silently farther and farther / from the waterfall to look up the side valleys and down / to the trail and climb to the crevices where he could see / the ridge." Such attentive and extended depiction of lonely, hunted, and alienated persons as *The Folding Cliffs* offers, becomes a way of fulfilling the charge Robert Hayden formulates as "visioning a world / where none is lonely, none hunted, alien."

The Folding Cliffs exemplifies one way in which poetry might have sa-
lubrious cultural and ecological effects. Activism may be coercive or persuasive. Both forms are needed, but they operate differently. Coercive activism operates on the *effects* of power relations. Strikers do not expect that
as a result of the strike management will share their views about the worth
of labor and the rights of laborers; they attempt to disrupt the connection
between current treatment of laborers and the profit of management. The
"argument" in a strike is: if you (management) continue to treat us (laborers) as you have been treating us, you will lose money; you will achieve
your aim of making money only by treating us differently. Persuasive activism operates on the *causes* of power relations. Management treats labor
the way it does as a result of commitment to certain assumptions about the
relative value of the subject's ownership of capital over the well-being and
satisfaction of other subjects, about entitlement to goods and privileges,
and so on. The "argument" in a poem (or other vehicle of persuasive activism) is that you should reconsider — and change — your assumptions.

Poetry may *support* coercive activism (as when strikers unite in chant-
ing or singing verse), but can itself engage only in persuasive activism. It
cannot withhold capital from the greedy, but it may alter the value judgments from which the greed of the greedy derives, so liberating them to
be other than greedy. In this way, poetry such as *The Folding Cliffs* may
be construed as pursuing what Slavoj Žižek identifies as our double task:
"to develop a theory of historical violence as something which cannot be
mastered/instrumentalized by any political agent, which threatens to en-
gulf this agent itself into a self-destructive vicious cycle, and... to pose the
question of 'civilizing' revolutions, of how to make the revolutionary process itself a 'civilizing' force."

The Folding Cliffs may be read, then, as an act of persuasive activism,
offering to readers a portrayal of an ideological dialectic: two antithetical
ideologies, the conflict between which can be reconciled only by a third,
synthetic, ideology. Its narrative of conflict between the antithetical ideologies offers the reader evidence of the greater healthfulness of, and an
opportunity to identify with and adopt, a synthetic ideology. The poem
does not coerce me into no longer enforcing by violent means the quarantine of persons with leprosy: I wasn't doing that anyway. It *does* persuade
me that my complicity in capitalist appropriation of "natural resources"

and transformation of those "resources" into goods and services available for my purchase might be unjust and cruel, harmful to myself, to other humans, and to the environment in which we live. In so persuading me, it also emboldens me to seek ways to minimize my complicity.

4.2: Poetry For Preparation

To the persuasive activism that attends a sound reading of W. S. Merwin's *The Folding Cliffs*, there correlate conditions for a sound reading.

Hamlet's Claudius "got it." During the performance Hamlet commissioned the players to give for the court, just after Lucianus poured poison in Gonzago's ear, Claudius rose and stopped the play, commanding, "Give me some light. Away!" In an alternative *Hamlet*, Claudius might have let the play continue, at its end explaining to Ophelia certain of its subtle Biblical allusions, and later discussing with Gertrude in their bedchamber clues to the psychological motivations of the characters, all lucidly and with clear conscience. But his explicating the play in this way, even with utmost accuracy, would only demonstrate that he had missed the point altogether. In the actual *Hamlet*, we don't know whether or not Claudius could have summarized the plot; his interrupting the play, though, shows that he got it. His getting it, in other words, is not contingent on his "understanding" the play as an ability to explain the play to others, identify literary devices at work in the play, and so on. Claudius might have a very full understanding in that sense, and still not get it at all. His getting it *is* contingent on his recognizing that, whatever else it may also be about, the play is about *him*. If he sees himself in the play, rightly ascertaining that Lucianus is him and he is Lucianus, and that he and Lucianus both are in the wrong, he gets it; if not, not.

There is at least one similarity between Claudius' viewing of the play and a contemporary reader's reading of W. S. Merwin's *The Folding Cliffs*. A reader of *The Folding Cliffs* will "get it" if and only if he/she correctly recognizes him- or herself in the poem, and arrives through that recognition at a clearer self-understanding.

In the early reception of a literary work, emphasis typically falls heavily on the question "Is it good?" There are reasons for this emphasis: reviews, for instance, function as gatekeepers, steering readers toward certain works and away from others. But its being *motivated* doesn't make emphasis on a question *ideal*. "Is it good?," asked as the primary question, the question that orients one's engagement, enervates the poem and trivializes the encounter with it. It suppresses the more crucial question, "What is at stake?," and settles in advance the reader's role and task.

Taking "Is it good?" as the primary question treats the poem as possessed of a (singular, settled) value, which I am to discern. I assume the role of judge, and the task of subjecting to an order the otherwise chaotic. I hold the poem up to a pre-set standard, and determine whether or not it matches. In an increasingly "global" society in which the privileged experience pluralism as a danger that culminates in terror and war, "Is it good?" is a tempting approach to the poem, because it settles the matter of inclusion in, or exclusion from, consideration. The ultimate fulfillment of the question "Is it good?" is canon-fixing, in which the status quo is secured by acknowledging and affirming what satisfies existing standards, and dismissing what does not.

"What is at stake?" does not settle in advance either my role or my task, but includes them within the question. "Is it good?" places me above the poem, makes it subject to my determination; "What is at stake?" sets me face-to-face with the poem, makes me just as subject to its determination as it is to mine. "Is it good?" is an aesthetic question; "What is at stake?" is an existential question. "Is it good?" is inherently monological and impositional, in contrast to the inherently dialogical and reciprocal "What is at stake?" "Is it good?" is a relatively closed and confining question, "What is at stake?" a relatively open and expansive question. Making "Is it good?" the primary question "puts the cart before the horse," and contributes to the liminality of poetry in our culture. A reliance on authority (she won the Pulitzer for her last book) rather than a willingness to judge for myself will be a likely result of asking "Is it good?" before asking what is at stake.

Early critical judgments of the worth of *The Folding Cliffs* (early answers to "Is it good?") diverged wildly. At one extreme, Michael Thurston offered lavish praise, saying that *The Folding Cliffs* "succeeds with power and grace." At the other, Adam Kirsch rebuked Merwin for reducing an "inherently powerful story" to mere tendentiousness by "flattening truth into myth."

Thurston's argument makes several points. First, he notes that *The Folding Cliffs* fills the last void in Merwin's otherwise complete and replete body of work. Merwin has written, he says, "in an astonishing variety of forms," including metrical verse and poetry in open forms, "prose memoirs and fiction, numerous translations, and even a verse drama." Until *The Folding Cliffs*, though, the long narrative poem has "been missing from [Merwin's] oeuvre." Secondly, *The Folding Cliffs*, Thurston observes, "enables Merwin to treat at length" a thematic concern that "has recurred throughout Merwin's career," namely "the pain and damage of separation and division." Thurston's third point heightens the praise: *The Folding Cliffs* inaugurates "a new poetic form, a form created through Merwin's reimagining of epic and narrative poetics." The reimagining is rooted in fulfillment of epic conventions: a beginning *in medias res*, inclusion of "embedded stories and genealogies," employment of "heightened diction," and development through "the slow accumulation of landmarks and recognizable relationships." But the theme of separation and division contrasts it to traditional epic, making it "a sort of anti-*Aeneid* for Hawai'i, an epic that treats not the founding of a city but the conquering, division, and dispersal of a people and its culture."

Kirsch's evaluation of *The Folding Cliffs* occurs as half of a review that also examines Merwin's collection *The River Sound*. Just as for Thurston *The Folding Cliffs* is representative, a culmination of Merwin's concerns, so for Kirsch *The Folding Cliffs* and *The River Sound* are representative, but rather than representing what is *good* about Merwin's work, they represent what is *bad*. The two together "furnish," Kirsch says, "a full look at Merwin's style and sensibility, his interests and the problems that they entail." Kirsch notes that Merwin explicitly avoids identifying *The Folding Cliffs* with either "the classical genre, the epic," or "the modern genre, the novel," preferring instead the more "neutral" status of "narrative," which commits only to the telling of a story without a concomitant commitment to *how* it will be told. The facts of the purportedly true story "comprise a strong and affecting tale," Kirsch says, that appeals to our cultural moment as "an ideal brief in the case against American colonialism." The poem's being so ideal a brief means that one cannot read it without "a renewed awareness of the brutality and the arrogance that were certified with the seal of 'manifest destiny.'" Its occasioning of such renewed awareness Kirsch calls a "lesson" that is part of "Merwin's didactic intention," but Kirsch excludes the lesson from the poem: it "has nothing to do with poetry, or indeed with literature. It is political, or historical, or humanitarian," but not poetic. The only pertinent issues, on Kirsch's view, are those "raised by its two aesthetic ambitions, the poetic and the novelistic." Kirsch does not explain how the poem maintains novelistic ambition in the face of its having ("appropriately," Kirsch opines) denied being a novel.

Given two such radically opposed assessments of the poem as those of Thurston and Kirsch, one might shrug and sigh that there's no accounting for tastes. You say tomayto, I say tomahto. But there's another possibility: that we *are* accountable for our tastes, and that the stakes in a work of art such as a poem (such as *this* poem) include that accountability. It may be, in other words, that judgment is *reciprocal*: in judging I am judged. The being judged occurs whether or not it is recognized, and whether or not it is acknowledged, by the person judging.

Consider as an analogy observations made by Louis Mackey about medieval proofs of God's existence. Proofs of God's existence present themselves, like judgments of poems, as accurate statements about an external reality. But Mackey points out that "not all who prove the existence of God are proving the same thing," and "not everyone who proves the existence of God is proving it in the same way"; from which it follows that, whether or not such proofs tell us anything about God, "the particular proof by which a philosopher chooses to demonstrate the existence of God tells us a great deal about his theological orientation and his philosophical disposition." Mackey's point is that, as there is in physics no absolute space to award objectivity to assessments of movement, so there is in philosophy no absolute indifference to award objectivity to assessments of truth: "Though they may claim to have no beliefs not validated by logic and the evidence, all philosophers are guided in their thinking by prior commitments, religious or irreligious, as much as they are by reason"; all "are trying to understand the world they *believe* they live in."

Similarly, each of the two example judgments of Merwin's poem tells us about the critical orientation and poetic disposition of the judge. Thurston's evaluation reveals his sense that a poem's success results from its achieving a satisfying concord between generic conventions and thematic concerns: the story "provides Merwin with a driving narrative and attractive characters" at the same time that it enables him to "treat at length" his recurring theme of division/separation. Kirsch's evaluation reveals that for him poetry is a strictly aesthetic phenomenon isolated from other human realms such as politics and history. The two precedents Kirsch names as having created successful long narrative poems on the basis of style alone are Wordsworth and Milton, either of whom would be surprised to see his poetry treated as a proof text for the exclusion of political, historical, and humanitarian concerns. Wordsworth, after all, claims of his "Lyrical Ballads" that "if the views with which they were composed were indeed realised," the poems will "interest mankind permanently" because of the quality and multiplicity of their "moral relations." In describing his plans for a poem to be called *The Recluse*, occasioned by *The Prelude* and with *The Excursion* as one of its parts, Wordsworth speaks of his "determination to compose a philosophical poem, containing views of Man, Nature, and Society." Milton, for his part, opens the first book of *Paradise Lost* with an invocation to the "Heav'nly Muse" to illumine the darkness in him, "That to the highth of this great Argument / I may assert Eternal Providence, / And justify the ways of God to men." Kirsch's desire to restrict poetry to style is flatly contradicted by his two exemplars: Wordsworth and Milton both claim for themselves and their poems "didactic intention," and claim such intention as an aspect of, not as something opposed to, the poems. For Wordsworth and Milton both, poetry is precisely what Kirsch says it isn't: political, historical, humanitarian, didactic.

Not all who ask whether a poem is good are asking the same thing. Thurston is asking about the adequacy of the poem to its own standards. "Is it good?" means to him something like "Does it employ conventions of genre in ways that aptly embody its themes?" Kirsch is asking about the adequacy of the poem to his standards. "Is it good?" means to him something like "Does it realize stylistic conventions I appreciate?" That Thurston and Kirsch apply different standards to the poem draws attention to the fact that the appropriate standard is not given but chosen; it is itself open to question. The choice of standard is a commitment intended to advance understanding of the world Thurston (or Kirsch) believes he lives in. I.e. the reader, like the standard, is involved in, rather than hovering outside of or above, the negotiation in reading the poem.

If "Is it good?" represents more than one question, if judgment is re-ciprocal, if standards and the reader are "in play" just as the poem is, then in addition to "Is it good?" we might do well to ask such other questions as "What good does it invite from me?" (As John F. Kennedy in his inaugural address invited Americans to "ask not what your country can do for you—ask what you can do for your country.") To what best aspect of me does it appeal? To what form of plenitude am I invited by the poem? Opening the standard question in this way draws attention to the complexity of the interaction between poem and reader. Thurston and Kirsch use their versions of "Is it good?" to foreclose other questions. So, for example, by calling *The Folding Cliffs* didactic (and taking didacticism as inherently bad and anti-poetic) Kirsch means that he finds the poem so far from fulfilling *his* standards that he refuses to entertain as a live question whether he fulfills the poem's standards. What he means by excluding historical or political content from poems is that his standards are the only ones that apply.

I suggest, though, that if the poem does fulfill its own standards but does not fulfill my standards, then a judicious spectator would ask what grounds there are for preferring one set of standards to the other, so questions about my standards all would be "live." "Is it good?" tests the poem's standards by mine, but "What is at stake?" tests my standards and the poem's standards against one another, treats them as inseparable, invites a dialogical rather than a monological reading. My claim here is that a reading that does not ask after *both* the poem's standards *and* my own standards is an empty reading, a reading that refuses the admonition that "You must revise your life," a reading that doesn't "get it."

In his response to *The Folding Cliffs*, John Burt makes a valuable distinction, between "verse which moves in the direction of conversation and verse which moves in the direction of music." The distinction arises, Burt contends, from verse's "dual allegiance... to talk and to chant." Burt himself employs the distinction to articulate how *The Folding Cliffs* does and does not fulfill its ambitions. Burt sees his distinction as "related but not identical to" that between narrative and lyric verse. Though narrative verse has been in decline, Burt notes that narrative and lyric "remain continuously engaged with one another," since lyric needs an implied narrative and narrative needs "moments of lyric intensity." But distinguishing between narrative and lyric verse is not enough for a reading of *The Folding Cliffs*, according to Burt, since, though *The Folding Cliffs* calls itself "A Narrative," it is *also*, Burt says, incantatory. Burt calls Merwin "a great contemporary master of chant," especially "when he seeks to set the foundation of his poem in the deepest stratum he can imagine."

Burt calls incantation "a technology for inducing a change in consciousness": to chant "is to work one's way into a special frame of mind separate from one's usual state, and to listen to a chant is to align oneself with that frame of mind." Talk seeks to "render people in their ordinariness," with normal motivations and capacities, but chant "lends itself to mythic character, to larger-than-life figures charged with *mana*, to characters who are embodied forces"; as embodied forces, they are "possessed by their acts and their feelings," in contrast to ordinary persons, who "make decisions under conditions of partial ignorance." Because characters in chant are mythic and possessed, incantation "seems not so much to depict them as to invoke them." Incantation seeks to be understood not as "the invention of its author's intelligence" but as "the incarnation of something which speaks through the author, something... deeper than personality, psychology, and biography." Its embeddedness in the ordinary means that talk "is always both heard and overheard, and the overhearing is part of the variegation which is its life." Chant closes that distance between hearing and overhearing: it "is never overheard in the way talk is overheard; one either gives oneself up to it or resists doing so." Chant tells mythic stories, so it allies itself with the epic, in contrast to talk, which tells timebound stories and therefore allies itself with history. Finally, chant is employed when a poem wishes "to align itself with tradition rather than modernity."

Alain Badiou stipulates a particular meaning of "truth," according to which a truth is "endowed with a transworldly and universal value," a "particular resistance" such that even though it occurs "in one world, it is valid *actually* for other worlds and *virtually* for all." A truth, though "produced with particular materials in a specific world," is "understood and usable in an entirely different world and across potentially vast spans of time." Truths, Badiou says, can migrate. Their "inviolate availability" makes it "possible for them to be resuscitated and reactivated in worlds heterogeneous to those in which they were created," and gives them the power of "crossing over, as such, unknown oceans and obscure millennia." Truths *apply*: "Incorporating yourself within a truth's becoming consists in bringing to the body serving as the support of this truth everything within you that has an intensity comparable to what it is that allows you to identify with the primordial statement." Truth happens when "degree of identity... is maximal." When Claudius sees that he is Lucianus, in other words.

What Badiou calls truth, I would call likeness. If my love can be like a red, red rose, then is it possible for W. S. Merwin to be like Pi'ilani? Is it possible for me? Perhaps more accurately, can I *regard* myself as like Pi'ilani, or *make* myself like Pi'ilani? The issue is not whether form and content relate properly (as Thurston affirms that they do) or whether purpose and genre relate properly (as Kirsch contends they do not), but whether my life and the poem relate properly. It is not self-evident that they *can* do so. The characters with whom we are invited to identify in *The Folding Cliffs*, including the protagonist, are Hawai'ian, not European or American. The protagonist is a female. W. S. Merwin is an American male, I am an American male, and everyone cited so far in this essay is a European or American male. As beneficiaries of wealth and security that were furthered by the Euro-American appropriation of Hawai'i, Merwin and I alike stand accused by the poem. That is, the poem's standards, according to which Europeans and Americans are the villains and Hawai'ians the victims and the heroes of the poem, conflict with standards that, even if neither of us would nominally accept them, created living conditions that privilege Merwin and me both.

As a narrative whose protagonist resists the colonialism being imposed on her, *The Folding Cliffs* puts at stake the limits of one's engagement with the other. A reader of the poem (at least readers who are citizens of colonizing nations, but also, I suggest, *any* reader) faces an ethical and civic question that could be formulated in this way: *Can I contain/diminish my (material) encroachment on the other, and release/expand my (spiritual) identification with the other?* It is not self-evident that it is possible to do so meaningfully. Such works as Gayatri Spivak's "Can the Subaltern Speak?" and J. M. Coetzee's *Elizabeth Costello* convey something of how problematic the question is. I have no answer to the question: argumentation and other discourse may help me find my way to an answer, but will not be itself the answer. A reading of *The Folding Cliffs*, though, might impose this (vital) question on me, and might also aid me as I seek to address the question.

Article 5:
Everything that descends must diverge.

5.1: Poetry Against Patriarchy

The myth of descent pervades western discourse, appearing already in ancient stories, as when Gilgamesh seeks Utnapishtim and when Odysseus consults the shade of Tiresias, entering Christian mythology as Christ's harrowing of hell, forming in medieval times the architecture of *Beowulf* and of Dante's *Inferno*, and informing such modernist literary works as T. S. Eliot's *The Waste Land*. To extra-literary culture it contributes such common metaphors as descent into poverty, descent into illness, descent into despair, and descent into madness. In Alice Notley's 1996 book-length poem *The Descent of Alette*, descent has a dual aspect: viewed as plot, Alette's descent is a journey; viewed as character, her descent is a metamorphosis. This dual aspect, the ability of either plot or character to bind the reader's gestalt, enables myth to critique both itself and the society in which it originates, thus enabling Alette's *descent* to be also an act of *dissent*.

Though the relations between literary categories in contemporary usage do not precisely match those that held in classical Greece, Aristotle's identification of the elements of tragedy offers a useful hermeneutic tool in regard not only to tragedy per se, but to all varieties of narrative. From most important to least, the elements are: *plot* (the combination of incidents); *character* (agents' moral purpose, what they seek or avoid); *thought* (what is shown in what the characters say); *diction* (the composition of the verses); *melody* (the tune to which the words are sung); and *spectacle* (the visual accompaniments of the performance, e.g. stage setting). Thought, diction, melody, and spectacle all serve plot and character, which are related inextricably. Plot, which consists in the protagonist's passing "from misfortune to happiness, or from happiness to misfortune," is best when it features a discovery, "a change from ignorance to knowledge, and thus to either love or hate, in the personages marked for good or evil fortune." Quality of plot and quality of character, in other words, are linked. External events and internal states reflect one another. The best tragic plots will be about a person "not preeminently virtuous and just, whose misfortune, however, is brought upon him not by vice and depravity but by some error of judgment."

Though Aristotle never says so, one reason for the primacy of plot and character is their ability to deliver a gestalt. In any narrative, the reader is tasked to arrive at some sense of the work as a whole. The other elements raise *why* questions that plot and character answer. Thought might ask why Antigone buries Polyneices and Eteocles; plot answers, because they were left unburied by Creon, and character, because Antigone is courageous. Spectacle asks why Antigone kneels when she buries Polyneices and Eteocles; plot answers, because she will later refuse to kneel before Creon, and character, because of her reverence. The gestalt offered by plot and character, though, begs to be more than the background facts, the story line, which is why a narrative such as *The Descent of Alette* resists simplifying summary. The back-cover description on Notley's book ("...a feminist epic, a bold journey into the deeper realms...") is profoundly inadequate to the poem. The richness of *The Descent of Alette*, as of any poem or narrative that bears scrutiny, derives in part from the fact that, because plot and character are reciprocal, a gestalt adequate to the text would account not only for plot or character separately, but also for their reciprocity.

As plot, a descent is one type of journey, the metaphysic of which is pessimistic: whether the protagonist overcomes or is overcome by her environment (whether she wins or loses, lives or dies) the forces of that environment are dark, and arrayed against her. (As compared to an ascent, a pilgrim's progress, in which the forces are ultimately benevolent.) The four books of *The Descent of Alette* correspond to the four stages of Alette's journey. In Book One, Alette passes through a subway system, and in Book Two through a network of caves. In Book Three she goes to a lake and meadow, and Book Four has her in the house of "the tyrant."

The first line of the first section of the first book of the poem places Alette within a journey, one that allusion to Dante tags as mythic. <"One day, I awoke" "& found myself on" "a subway, endlessly">. Alette professes not to know <"how I'd arrived there or" "who I was" "exactly">, though she does recognize herself as within a plot: <"...I knew the train" "knew riding it">. She is also already aware, even within that first section, of the existence of "the tyrant," and his role as <"a man in charge of" "the fact" "that we were" / "below the ground" "endlessly riding" "our trains, never surfacing">; through that awareness, the reader is initiated into the poem's pessimistic metaphysic, divining already that the forces of Alette's environment are dark.

Alette becomes increasingly preoccupied with the tyrant. She receives conflicting accounts of his nature and identity, which she must try to sort out. The accounts, all fragmentary, include events attributed to the tyrant's personal history, as when Alette is told that once, <" 'years ago, the tyrant" "was shot">. They also include sweeping statements about the tyrant's character and powers, as when Alette is told that <"The tyrant" "owns form"">. Alette understands that the tyrant is connected to her own situation in a deeply problematic way, and suffers <"Despair & outrage"> as she realizes the equivalence of her riding a <"mechanical contrivance" "in the darkness"> and her being steeped in <"the authority" // "of" "another's mind" "the tyrant's mind">. But she also understands that such connection to the tyrant implies also a different kind of connection, a form of solidarity, with others. Alette accepts and shares the point of view she is presented with by another subway passenger, that the passengers' fates cannot be separated: <"I can't leave it [the subway]" "ever" "unless" / "we all leave—' ">. That collective fate is governed by the laws of the inverted, subterranean world through which Alette journeys. <"We can only go" "down" "farther down —">, Alette is told. <"Down" "is now the only way" "to rise">.

However, Alette does not trust all the reports she receives. On one occasion, presented with a "ghoulish" man as the tyrant, she sees through the deception. <"He's not the tyrant"> she tells the man who presents the ghoulish figure to her, <"He's a simple // ghoul" "The tyrant" "is a mild-" "looking man" "He does not show" / "his decay" "He has no such grace," "you might say">. The tyrant, though, will not be easily mastered, nor his disguises all easily seen through. Soon after Alette's dismissal of the ghoulish man, she encounters a friendly-looking old man, whose cheek she pats. She has been talking to another man, who at that moment, in identifying the tyrant to her, delineates explicitly for the first time in the poem the quest Alette must undertake: <"The man said," " 'You've just patted" "the cheek of" / "the man" "you must confront" "& vanquish' ">. Alette receives her formal charge in the next section, from a huge owl that visits the car in which Alette is riding. <"I've come here" "to say" "that when you finally" "meet with / the tyrant —" "do you know yet" "you must confront him?' ">. Alette asks what she is being charged to do, and is told that the tyrant must die. Her objection that she can't kill someone is overruled: <"You // are an animal,' said the owl," " 'an animal" "as I am" "Act like / an animal" "when you kill him" "As little" "as possible" / "must happen" "It must be clean.' "> Her task has been presented as it would be presented in Greek epic, by a god in the shape of an animal (Athena often takes the shape specifically of an owl), and that avatar promises to help the protagonist through a conflict that otherwise exceeds the mortal's resources. Unlike the heroes in the *Iliad*, though, who vaunt their prowess, Alette is self-effacing. <" 'I have no prowess,' I said">.

Book One ends with the train's dissolution: <"Its sides fall away" "I am floating" "There is / nothing" "but the dark" "everywhere" "around me">. Book Two opens with Alette reporting that <"I floated" "down in darkness" "among" "the other bodiless" / "people" "from the black train">, until eventually <"I lost sense of other presences," "felt nearly" "non- / existent">, but saw a mountain in the distance, and headed <"for the mountain" "in a gradual" "downward arc —">. Alette finds herself in <"a cave that was" "a sort of" "antechamber"> with a door <"which seemed to lead towards other caves">. Seeking orientation from the "maintenance man" who is there, she is given an imperative. <" 'Can you tell me" "more clearly" // "what these caves are?'>, Alette asks. He replies that they are like <"our middle depths" "or middle psyche, if you prefer">, and he instructs her, <"Now get on with" // "your journey'">. Which Alette does, stepping through the door into the next cave.

Neither her early denial of prowess nor her reticence about killing the tyrant implies lack of courage or will. As the struggle with the tyrant intensifies, so does Alette's commitment. She does not allow herself to be cowed. At one point during her passage through the caves, a portrait of the tyrant comes alive and speaks to her, charging her, <" 'Don't walk through" "the tunnel">, and threatening her, <"At the end of / it" "you will die">. Her reply, far from timid or acquiescent, is defiant. <" 'This tunnel" "represents" / "my whole journey, doesn't it?' " "— I called back to" "the tyrant" // " 'Well I'm going to" "see it through' ">. Seeing the journey through depends sometimes on agency, but sometimes on patience. When she enters a cave <"whose walls closed up" "around me," "until" / "it became" "exactly my size, my body's size">, Alette's response is not to struggle against the entrapment, but to observe a small turquoise blue salamander that climbs onto her shoulder, to feel the hollow shiver it provokes, and finally to fall asleep. The map onto which she falls in her dream becomes <"a field of" "snow at night" // "cold & cleansing">, and Alette awakens, restored: <"my room was larger," / "had a door &" "I was plural," "was others," "was my companions" "again">.

Though one purpose of her journey (killing the tyrant) has been imposed on her, Alette also maintains a self-imposed purpose, namely looking for <"A lost" "first mother," "an Eve / unlike Eve," "or anyone" "whose name we know' ">. Maintaining her own purpose for the journey does not relieve Alette of the imposed purpose, which she does not try to escape: <" 'I will / do it,' I said" " 'You want me, don't you," "to kill the tyrant?" // "I will kill him">. She knows, though, that <"...it won't happen" "quite yet"> because <"I have to / journey first" "farther down" "into this darkness' ">. Continuing her journey, Alette leaves the caves, following a voice that instructs her to keep walking through a long corridor. She walks, <"surmising" "that I was about" "to exit" "this whole system" // "of caves">. She descends a staircase, mysteriously lit so that only the steps directly in front of her are visible. The staircase empties onto a riverbank at night, and Alette follows the voice's reiterated instruction to keep walking. <"I walked to" / "the river's edge," "took off my shoes," "left them there" // "Began to wade" "into the water"> that defines the geography of Book Three.

After crossing a river, passing through woods, and visiting a meadow, Alette is led by her owl guide to a gazebo at the edge of a lake. She asks him what lake it is, and he answers, <" 'I find it difficult" / "to define" "It is the center" "of the deep..." "Of this underworld, / I guess">. Pursuing the question, Alette receives another affirmation that the topos through which she journeys is simultaneously an outer and an inner landscape. <" 'How deep is it?' I asked" " 'Infinitely" "deep,' he said" " 'It // connects with" "the great darkness," "connects with" "one's death—' ">. Only after death (she is eaten by the owl) and receipt of a "death body" is Alette led to the tyrant's house by the owl. She climbs up through a hole into the basement, and the owl leaves her there; he descends again, and leaves her to rise. Alette meets the tyrant immediately upon entering his house, but long dialogue precedes the actual physical conflict through which Alette kills him. He warns her that he is <"not vulnerable" "at all,"> and indeed claims <" 'I'm not even" "a real person' ">. He feigns puzzlement — <"You didn't" "really think" "you could kill me," "just // kill me?"> — and laughs at her, then becomes almost cordial. <" 'Come tour" "my house with me,' / he said" " 'You can't kill me;" "so join me" "for now'">.

The final act of the journey as plot is to remind us of the journey as character. Alette's journey through the world transforms the very world through which she journeys. When she returns to the world above the subway, the street is <"filling up" "with people"> who <"...knew he must be dead"> and stand <"...staring into" "the clear air:">. They see a <"jeweled blue"> sky, and know that they can now have <"...infinity" "in our lives">. As a result of Alette's descent, <"The light has been made new' ">.

As plot, descent is a journey; as character, descent is a metamorphosis, a change of internal state that expresses itself outwardly. (As compared to ascent, which is a miracle, a change of external conditions that renews the inner person.) In the course of her journey, Alette undergoes a series of metamorphoses that sum to one large-scale metamorphosis, the realization of freedom that is the equivalent of her fulfilling the quest. As journey, Alette escapes from physical confinement; as metamorphosis, Alette is spiritually liberated (and liberates others).

The metamorphoses are often modes of resistance to the current state. For instance, one metamorphosis that Alette observes (rather than undergoing herself) is illegal. A woman begins stripping for money, and as she takes off her blouse, she begins to grow feathers, <"& by the time she was naked," "she wore the / head" "of an eagle" "a crowned eagle" "a raptor" "herself —" / "And as she stood" "& faced the car" "her body" "was changing" // "was becoming entirely" "that bird" "those wings,"> but the authorities intervene. <"A cop came" / "As if ready" " as if they knew" "Her wings were clipped," // "talons cut" "as if as quickly as possible">. The woman's illegal metamorphosis into an eagle presages Alette's own metamorphosis into an owl, which will allow Alette to kill the tyrant in Book Four.

If the tyrant, viewed through plot, is the object of Alette's journey, he is also, viewed through character, the occasion of at least some of her metamorphoses. For example, in one section, Alette observes the tyrant in ghostly form encasing other passengers in her subway car, and then he begins to encase her, causing a metamorphosis she has to resist. <"He sank down" "into my head" "into my thoughts," / "which instantly" "separated" "assumed a terrifying" "strict // order" "unfamiliar" "to me" "Each felt distinct" "from each">, a condition which Alette resists in part because <"No thought felt true">. The connection between journey and metamorphosis is especially explicit in the transition from Book One to Book Two. As journey, <"This particular" "train" "will leave the subway" / "for another," "deeper," "unilluminated place," "where all is" / "uncharted">; as metamorphosis, <"All will" "become a darkness" "in which each of you" "will also / lose form">. As the train pulls away, Alette's questions reveal concerns about both plot and character: <"Where" "are we going?" "Will I be there?" "Who am I now?">.

That the metamorphoses Alette undergoes are physical manifestations of spiritual conditions is often made explicit, as when Alette notices that a small drop of a white substance she identifies as evil <"oozed" "from my palm">. Alette connects the white substance to war, and disclaims complicity with it. <" 'I've never" "been to war" "I've never" "been allowed" // "to participate" "in the decision to go to war —' ">, she protests. <" 'I've done nothing,' I said" " 'Has someone" "such power" // "as to make his sin" "ooze from my pores?' ">. The metamorphoses also occur as literalizings of identification with others. At one point during her time in the caves in Book Two, Alette stands before three paintings painted onto the cave walls, one of them a portrait of a nude woman with a black hole where her face should be. Alette feels herself becoming the woman. <"I began to weep —">, she says. <"I wasn't" "sad inside," "but I wept & wept" / "A roaring" "sucking wind" "began blowing" "all around me" "The room / darkened;" "I stood suddenly" "inside the" "painted woman," / "stood nude inside" "her dark facelessness."> So complete is Alette's identification with the woman that <"I had" "become her">.

In the next cave she visits, Alette is again metamorphosed, this time not through purity of identification, but through division. In this cave, <"...I instantly" "divided into three" / "separate" "figures," "chained together" "in single file">. This metamorphosis is temporal. When she asks <" 'Why are there three of me" "in here?'>, she is (they are) told <" 'You are your" "Past, Present," "& Future'>. A man gives her this information, but by the end of the poem she is teaching him. He asks if she is going forward, and warns her that death lies ahead. She is not intimidated. <" 'Any woman" "may already" "be dead,' "> she tells him: <"No remembrance" "of our mother" / "No remembrance" "of who we really are" "Thus a woman" "may be" / "already dead" "born dead">.

We might expect metamorphoses to function metaphorically or allegorically, but the section beginning <"I entered" "a cave"> shows the ease with which the metamorphoses in *Alette* also work allusively. Alette enters into a conversation with a woman who has turned into rock. The woman's complaint is of the violence of patriarchal power structures, and the section manages, without making any allusion explicit, to allude to Plato's allegory of the cave (by the location of the conversation), the Vietnam Veterans' Memorial in Washington, D.C. (<" 'We'll carve'" "his name,' / she said," " 'into a wall'" "where there are so" "many names">), Michelangelo's "Pietà," and by extension other artists' pietàs, and by further extension the gospel narratives of Christ's burial. Such allusive metamorphosis does not exclude metaphorical or allegorical metamorphosis, another example of which occurs just three pages later, when another woman turns into stone, but this time in such a way that she <"became" "herself cavelike">, freezing <"into a model of" / "caves like the caves" "we stood in">, and leading Alette to fear that <"...I stood" "exactly" "inside of" "women's bodies"> and to ask <"Was"/ "the human psyche" "made of women" "turned to stone?...">.

Change can be a source of hope, as when Alette reports that <"I was alone" "Myself &" "alone" "Yet emptied" "of much, it seemed" / "I felt unburdened" "& even buoyant">. It can also be a cause of fear, as when Alette meets a headless woman who asks her to sit <"for a minute" "enjoying this night" / "before we change" "Change forever">. When Alette reunites the woman's head to her body, she (the woman) becomes the first mother: <"her face" "began to change" / "Color" "poured into it">, she became younger than Alette <"& yet she was, I felt," "truly" "our mother...">. Alette's own metamorphoses and those of the other presences are not random and isolated, but interconnected and recursive. The formerly headless woman returns soon, <"as a spirit" "with a snake's" // "lower body">, and enters Alette through her mouth, after which Alette dreams she floats in air, and awakens in <"a new clearing," / "brightly lit">. Each metamorphosis prepares for the next. After the owl eats her, Alette asks how it is that she is not dead, and is told that <"parts of your insubstantial / body —" "have been" "replaced" "The owl replaced them">. <"You are now equipped">, Alette is assured, <"to experience" "what you need'">.

Told that in the tyrant's world, what she will need is to fly alone, Alette asks, <" 'I will fly?'>. The owl assures her that <" 'You are owl,'>, a metamorphosis that indeed proves necessary. At one point while walking with the tyrant Alette is invited to cross over a stretch of abandoned subway track covered with rats. It is too far for her to simply step or leap over, but she successfully crosses, and when she reaches the other side the tyrant tells her <" 'You became an owl,' ">, <"& you flew" "You flew across' ">. The poem's final metamorphosis is not one Alette *experiences*, but one she *accomplishes*. As a result of Alette's killing the tyrant, another woman is able to fold his body into <"a small square shape"> that she simply lays aside, and those who have been underground are freed to return to the light: <"all the // lost creatures" "began to" "emerge" "Come up from" "below the subway" / "From the caves &" "from the dark woods" "I had visited">. At the book's conclusion, a utopian unity and inclusion is achieved, at least briefly. <"Whatever," "whoever," "could be," "was possible," "or / had been" "forgotten" "for long ages" "now joined us," "now / joined us once more," "Came to light" "that morning">.

In her "Author's Note," Notley claims bluntly that "I am not Alette." But even so apparently simple a statement might have more than one meaning, and the statement does not mean that Alette has a singular identity distinct from Notley's. It means that Alette is not only Notley, but also the rest of us, Notley herself included. Notley does not stand for us all, but Alette does. She is an *ethos* (Aristotle's word for "character") rather than a human individual, and her metamorphoses belong to Notley no more nor less than they do to others.

It would be impossible even to flip through the pages of *The Descent of Alette* without noticing that every line in the nearly 150 pages of poetry is broken into shorter phrases by quotation marks. Notley's "Author's Note" at the beginning of the book gives a rationale. "[T]hey're there, mostly," Notley says of the quotation marks, "to measure the poem." The end of the author's note asserts the poem's narrativity: "this is not a thought, or a record of thought-process, this is a story, told." By juxtaposing a statement of the poem's subjection to measurement with a claim for the poem's narrative status, Notley raises a question: why must this story be measured in the telling? Notley's answer in the author's note has to do with pace and distance. "The quotation marks make the reader slow down and silently articulate — not slur over mentally — the phrases at the pace, and with the stresses, I intend. They also distance the narrative from myself, the author." Though the rationale Notley offers is not *wrong*, neither is it exhaustive. At least one other aspect of the quotation marks is that they function as scare quotes, implicitly qualifying and "ironicizing" the poem. In this way they are of a piece with the poem's critical posture.

"To measure the poem" is not for Notley a dislocated or arbitrary ideal. Aristotle's identification of the elements of tragedy is for him one step in an argument for tragedy's superiority over epic, and Notley's sense of measure in *Alette* is one part of the book's appeal to, and simultaneous critique of, epic. In her essay "Homer's *Art*," Notley identifies measure as crucial to Homer. "Homer's *Art*," Notley contends, "is to tell a public story, in a measure that makes that possible," that offers "a pleasure in the music as the truth of its telling," so that "as the story is told in this measure it becomes really true — the measure draws from the poet depths of thought & feeling, as well as memory." This observation leads Notley to what might be taken as a statement of purpose for *Alette*. Homer's stories are "stories for men about a male world," and helped establish as "the epitome of achievement in Western poetry" the epic, a "large long story" about a war, written by men who "have tended, or tried, to be near the center of the politics of their time, court or capital."

So what, Notley asks, happens if one is a woman and "someone you know dies many years after the Vietnam War" (our "strange faraway but shattering" equivalent of the Trojan War)? "To tell that story, which is both personal & very public, you might distance it from yourself, somehow, & find a sound for it — as the Greeks did — that makes your telling of it listenable to & true." That gendered/political ideal has a corresponding aesthetic ideal, "to steal story away from the novel & give it back to rhythm & sound, give it back to the line." Writing in the direction of those ideals, "a long poem, a story poem, with a female narrator/hero" might help to recover "some sense of what mind was like before Homer, before the world went haywire & women were denied participation in the design & making of it," might even help someone to "discover that original mind inside herself now, in these times." Just such a service to poetry (a critical service, a critique both of epic itself and of the society in which it originates) Notley seeks to perform. *The Descent of Alette* participates in a broader questioning of the narrative valorizing of war and masculinity: "there is no one history," Miriam Cooke contends, "no one story about war, that has greater claim to truth." Instead, "history is made up of multiple stories, many of them herstories." *The Descent of Alette* is one such herstory.

In this way page 73 of *The Descent of Alette* represents the effect of the quotation marks. When the speaker says <"Phrases" "were repeated," "almost sung, / choruslike">, that might be a way to speak of the effect of the quotation marks. A phrase sung, rather than read, becomes choruslike, in the sense of the ancient Greek chorus. This poem, <"I found" "a room of voices" "It was a cave of" "small containers">, is mythic like the rest of *The Descent of Alette*. The small containers each containing a voice <"which emerged in" "a line of white smoke" / "& spoke" "in midair"> lead to the larger container: <"It was a black urn" "& its voice arose" "in a grayer / smoke" "It spoke" "in a rich" "female whisper:">. So it becomes like the Delphic Oracle, another female voice arising from the earth with a rich female whisper, and uttering oracular pronouncements. Notley's speaker asks all the voices, not only the voice from the black urn, to say <*"Whatever" "is frozen" "will now melt"*>, and the voices do say, as the speaker requested, <" 'It will melt" "it will melt now" "will melt,' they" "began to chorus" / " 'Whatever's frozen" "will now melt...' ">.

Chorus and oracle alike raise the stakes. They link plot and character (external and internal, journey and metamorphosis), establishing their reciprocity. The oracle is divine, but must be divined. The chorus recognizes that knowledge of the course of events does not untie that course from character. Notley's quotation marks invest the poem with the same ironic distance and resistance. What Notley calls measure is the reciprocity of plot and character; it raises the stakes for the gestalt by distinguishing the parts more fully, thus making the assembly of the whole more dramatic. Assembly of the whole, after all, is needed. Plot cannot be adequate in itself. I have completed my journey (made my million bucks, won fame, bought that BMW): so what? Without a change of internal state, the external events have no meaning. Similarly, character cannot be adequate in itself. I found inner peace, but orphans still suffer in Sudan. Without a change in external events, internal change has no value. Plot and character critique each other, and complement each other: change in the external shows the inadequacy of, and the need for, change in the internal, and vice versa. One human project is to invite such reciprocity (simultaneous critique and complementarity) between the enclosed self (one's character, one's internal state) and the porous self (one's journey, one's effects on/in the world). Narrative is a mode of invitation to such reciprocity, an act of assent and dissent alike. Alice Notley's Alette ascends and assents only after (and because) she descends and dissents, invoking a myth to reiterate the human.

5.2: Poetry Against Tyranny

In the study of literature, "close reading" operates as an unassailable, the way "free market" operates in contemporary political discourse. So for example even as he makes the case for an alternative approach to reading, one he names "globalectics," Ngũgĩ wa Thiong'o still nods to "the close reading of texts (which I value to this day)." The valuation seems self-evident: *of course* it's good for the market to be free; *of course* it's good to read closely. But in fact the efficiency of the market depends on constraint as much as it depends on freedom: unregulated markets concentrate wealth ever more exclusively in the hands of a very few, creating widespread poverty and structural violence. Similarly, a close reading might be "close" in the negative sense of that term, according to which what is close is stifling. In recognition of that qualification, this inquiry into Alice Notley's *The Descent of Alette* will *not* perform a "close reading." Instead, it will read in a manner much more like Ngũgĩ's proposed "globalectic" reading, his "way of approaching any text from whatever times and places allow its contents and themes [to] form a free conversation with other texts."

I take as my starting point a statement from Notley herself. Near the end of her short essay "Women and Poetry," an exact contemporary of *Alette*, Notley makes this declaration:

> Finally we [women] are allowed to write but the world is dying — the poems are dying — the literal ones I mean, at least seemingly. In this ridiculous inescapable and tawdry material world we women are allowed now what? To make more of it, more of that, more stuff. But not to remake it. Not to change it from the ground up and walk out onto the earth as if it were its first morning. Walk out and see being all around us, see the real poems. The sons-of-bitches in Washington and Wall Street and L.A. are still sons and rich ones — admitting a few exactly like-minded bitches — and worse, still self-perpetuatingly powerful in the tiny glassed-in bubble that contains all the master controls. Very few people, male or female,

seem capable of making a life that doesn't conform to the patterns that so benefit these tyrants.

This passage reads like a "mission statement" or "declaration of purpose" for *The Descent of Alette*, obviously because it resists tyrants, but also because it foregrounds two purposes (to remake, and to not conform) that well characterize *The Descent of Alette*. The *pre*scriptions in the prose passage work as *de*scriptions of the poem. In *Alette* the material world is remade, changed from the ground up (even from *under*ground up), so completely that at poem's end Alette "walk[s] out onto the earth as if it were the first morning." In so doing, *Alette* refuses to conform to the patterns that benefit the tyrants. That is to say, Alette's *descent* is also *dissent*.

For the sake of argument, grant this as a description of the purpose of *Alette*, its end. One might grant it in either of two senses: a skeptical reader, convinced that "poetry makes nothing happen," might grant that *Alette aims* to remake the material world, etc.; a more generous reader might grant the stronger claim that *Alette achieves* the remaking, etc. In either case, granting as the *end* of *Alette* a remaking of the material world and a refusal to conform to patterns that serve tyrants invites asking after the *means* by which that end is pursued and/or achieved. In the preceding chapter, I sought to articulate this means in terms of the *mythos* of the poem. Here, I will frame it in terms of the *logos* of the poem. Toward a reading that is more "globalectic" than "close," I will "step back" from *Alette*, to consider it contextually and comparatively, by way of contrast with two other descents familiar from literary history, arguing that *Alette*, by insisting on the reality of, and operating in the space of, the gap between enacted justice and ideal Justice, rejects the cultural and political status quo by denying the metaphysical sanction typically applied as an enforcement mechanism. Those other two descents, Dante's *Inferno* and Plato's allegory of the cave, affirm the status quo with an ultimate, metaphysical, affirmation: *Alette* performs its dissent by rejecting the "real" world status quo in favor of an alternative metaphysical world.

Alette itself invites the comparison with (and contrast to) the *Inferno*, by echoing Dante's first line in its own. Notley's < "One day, I awoke" "& found myself on" "a subway, endlessly" > evokes Dante's "In the middle of the journey of our life, I awoke in a dark wood." To that invited comparison/contrast I add another, one that the text doesn't invite quite so explicitly, but that, as I argue, it sustains, namely with Plato's allegory of the cave. The feature of *Alette* that I highlight by this double comparison is its refusal of a form of piety for which I here coin the term *cosmotism*. The comparison shows that the descent into Dante's hell and the descent into Plato's cave affirm the status quo in the most profound possible way, and that the descent into Notley's subway withholds that ultimate affirmation. This withholding is a mode of dissent.

I arrive at the terms *cosmot* and *cosmotic* and *cosmotism* by analogy with *patriot* and *patriotic* and *patriotism*. *Patriot* arrives in English from the Latin *patriota*, itself derived from the Greek *patriotes*, which comes from *patrios*, the genitive form of *patris*, the noun meaning fatherland. A patriot is one who affirms her or his nation unconditionally, who identifies with her/his nation without reserve. (That unreserved affirmation and identification includes the nation's projected masculinity, so neatly captured by the Greek *patris*, a cognate of *pater*, the word for father.) By analogy, I derive *cosmotism* from the Greek *cosmos*, the universe, the order of things. If a patriot affirms her *patris* unconditionally, a cosmot affirms the cosmos unconditionally. A patriot embraces, and defends, the local, *political* status quo; a cosmot embraces and defends the cosmic, *metaphysical* status quo.

Critiques of patriotism take various approaches. George Kateb argues that patriotism fails because it lacks self-restraint. "The highest moral principles," he says, "teach restraint of self-preference, whether the self is oneself or a group-self." But patriotism, like nationalism, is a form of "group narcissism without any self-restraint except for a frequently unreliable prudence, and carried to death-dealing lengths." Stan van Hooft's critique, too, identifies patriotism's resemblence to nationalism as problematic. Both patriotism and nationalism arise from a misjudgment: "the special focus on one's country that they espouse elevates that country into having an importance of its own." A patriot judges that the nation is more important than human rights and social justice on a global scale, when in fact, van Hooft contends, that order of importance ought to be reversed.

To such critiques of patriotism might be added another, one that helps reveal the dissent in *Alette*. A dissident recognizes a gap that a patriot does not admit. The gap is not the subjective gap, articulated by Harry Frankfurt, to which van Hooft appeals in his critique of patriotism. Frankfurt identifies "second-order desires" as peculiar to humans. "Many animals appear to have the capacity for what I shall call 'first-order desires' or 'desires of the first order,' which are simply desires to do or not to do one thing or another. No animal other than man, however, appears to have the capacity for reflective self-evaluation that is manifested in the formation of second-order desires." Second-order desires enable us to do what members of other species cannot, namely to want to be "different, in [our] preferences and purposes, from what [we] are." Van Hooft sees second-order desires as enabling ironic commitments, of the sort a fan has for her favorite sports team, as compared to her non-ironic commitment to her spouse. The patriot's mistake is subjective and attitudinal, a failure to exercise second-order desire. A patriot is mistaken in maintaining non-ironic, rather than ironic, commitment to her nation.

The critique of patriotism most relevant to the dissent in *Alette*, though, is not subjective but objective. It has to do not primarily with the maintenance of internal gap, but with the recognition of an external one, the gap between the ideal and the real. In the U.S., to choose one example, much is made of the ideal of "liberty and justice for all." To a patriotic American, that ideal is realized in and by the United States. To a dissident, though, the ideal is not yet realized, or not yet fully realized: such phenomena as the wealth gap between men and women, and the fact that no woman has yet been President (never mind the nation's official sanction of torture, its unchecked surveillance, and on and on) suggest that the actual policies, practices, and institutions of the nation do not live up to its stated ideals. This gap between ideal and real is the space of civil disobedience. When Henry David Thoreau expresses dissent by refusing to pay his poll taxes, he is marking the gap between ideal ("liberty and justice for all") and real (U.S. participation in the Mexican-American War and state sanction of slavery). When the Constable of Concord puts Thoreau in jail, in his patriotism he denies the reality of that gap. When Martin Luther King, Jr. expresses dissent by participating with the Southern Christian Leadership Conference in demonstrations, he is marking the gap between ideal ("liberty and justice for all") and real (racial segregation). When the Birmingham police jail him, in their patriotism they deny the reality of that gap.

In the political realm, a dissident marks what a patriot denies: a difference between how things are and how they ought to be. The U.S. Pledge of Allegiance precedes its *patriotic* affirmation, "with liberty and justice for all," with a *cosmotic* affirmation, "one nation, *under God.*" The patriot's identification of her/his political group with Justice finds support from the cosmot's closure of the gap between justice and Justice, the erasure of any difference between how things are and how they ought to be. Conversely, the dissident's political *distinction* between nation and Justice testifies to the metaphysical distinction between how things are and how they ought to be. (This is why political conservatism and religious fundamentalism so consistently ally themselves.)

Consider now the descents from literary history with which I am contrasting *Alette*. Anthony K. Cassell asserts that, even though Dante uses the term *contrapasso* "but once in all his works," yet "the concept of the *contrapasso* is at the centre of the Poet's whole creation of Hell, philosophically, and artistically." Cassell defines *contrapasso* as "the justice of retaliatory punishment," and identifies as Dante's source for the concept Aquinas, for whom, Cassell says, *contrapasso* "denotes equal suffering in repayment for previous action;... for instance, if a man strike, that he be struck back." Dante uses the term only once, but the concept is the generative principle of the *Inferno*. The frame narrative sustains instance after instance of this type of poetic justice, in which a wrong done returns to the wrongdoer in a form analogous to the wrong itself. To give only one example, in Canto V, Dante hears the "groaning, tears, laments" of those (Cleopatra, Helen, Paris, et al.) who "sinned in carnal things." Because on earth they allowed turbulent desire to master calm, ordered reason, in hell they suffer perpetual turbulence: "Turbulent in a storm of warring winds, / The hurricane of Hell in perpetual motion // Sweeping the ravaged spirits as it rends, / Twists, and torments them." As they did in the first life, so they are done unto in the second.

In the *Inferno*, this correlation between vice and punishment manifests itself not only in the individual punishments meted out to individual souls, but also in the very structure of hell itself. In Canto XI, for example, Virgil explains to Dante as they enter the sixth circle that "Within these rocks three lesser circles fall, // Each one below another" according to rules that "Determine how and why they are constrained." The rules are such as this one: injustices committed by force and those committed by fraud both are wrong, as Virgil explains, but "since fraud is found // In humankind as its peculiar vice, / It angers God more: so the fraudulent / Are lower, and suffer more unhappiness." Hell is arranged in such a way that the worse the sin, the deeper the placement of those who committed it. Hell has — or just *is* — a moral topography: its material organization manifests the moral organization of the cosmos. The *Inferno*, then, is an unremittingly cosmic work: in it, Justice reigns without compromise or qualification. By divine necessity, a person's (internal) *state* and his or her (external) *condition* match precisely. A person's decisions and actions always bring about results that mirror them exactly. The cosmos is exactly as it should be. What is, what must be, and what ought to be match. My material conditions ultimately reflect my nature. As I erred, so I suffer. The relationship between action and consequence is settled, correlative, unconditional, *perfect*. No political activity is incumbent upon us, nor could political activity have effect. Conservatism is appropriate because the status quo is the best of all possible worlds.

The same holds for the other comparator descent, Plato's allegory of the cave, with this difference: the perfection of the relationship between action and consequence is fulfilled *externally* in Dante, by material conditions, but *internally* in Plato, by spiritual condition. Unlike the *Inferno* and *Alette*, the allegory of the cave is not a work unto itself. Though often read in isolation, it is a small part of a much larger work, the *Republic*. That larger work (in which the allegory of the cave occurs fairly late, in Book 7 of a work with 10 books), is all about the question, posed in Book 1, Why should humans be good? Socrates and his friends engage in conversation with a wealthy old man, Cephalus, who, asked whether his money made him happy, replies that money is ok, but the real issue is whether one has lived a just life. This response leads the others into a discussion of what justice is and why one should pursue it.

If that is the global issue of the *Republic*, the more local, immediate puzzle Socrates is trying to solve is posed by a parable, the Gyges ring story, told by one of Socrates' interlocutors, Glaucon. In it, the shepherd Gyges discovers a ring that gives him the power to be invisible at will, and thus to get away with anything he wants. Using that power, he insinuates himself into the court, seduces the queen, kills the king, and becomes king himself.

Glaucon takes it as obvious that *any* of us would, like Gyges, abuse the power of invisibility in service of unmitigated self-interest. The Gyges ring story shows, as Glaucon understands it, not only that humans all would choose *not* to be accountable if that choice were permitted us, but also that such permission is denied us only by social consensus, not by nature. The ring makes Gyges invisible to other humans, not to the gods. *Euphrosyne* (happiness) is tied to *dikaiosyne* (justice) only by a socially-constructed cord. We are punished by *society* if we act unjustly, but not by the *cosmos*. Any dependence of euphrosyne on dikaiosyne is extrinsic, not intrinsic, and their having only extrinsic connection leaves it to be the case that the more *in*justice we can get away with, the happier we are.

So Glaucon thinks, but the allegory of the cave is a part of Socrates' argument *against* Glaucon's hypothesis. Socrates contends that euphrosyne depends on dikaiosyne *intrinsically*. His argument is that you might *think* you're happy if you're rich and unjust, but you're not; and you might *think* someone else is happy if they're rich and unjust, but they're not. His case reflects (and extends) the Greek concepts of *euphrosyne* and *dikaiosyne*, which, though usually translated as *happiness* and *justice*, are less like "feeling good" and "following the rules" than they are like consonance with how things are, reflected in one's condition and in one's actions. Such consonance is good if and only if *how things are* is good. Plato's claim is not (like Dante's) that an external force (God) imposes Justice by correlating material conditions with spiritual state, but that a sound spiritual state needs no material correlative. It is complete in itself; its completion is not completion *by* material conditions. The allegory of the cave, in other words, is intended to assert that we should be good not for extrinsic reasons (coercion, the threat of punishment, etc.), but for intrinsic reasons (who we are, what the good is). The point is not that there is in fact another world, but that if we recognize this world for what it is, if we see *sub specie aeternitatis* instead of *sub specie humanitatis*, if we see things as a god would see things, if we recognize them, see them as they are, then we see that we cannot have euphrosyne without dikaiosyne, i.e. we cannot have what is ours if others do not have what is rightfully theirs. To recognize things for what they are, to see as a god would see, *is* Justice. Plato's view internalizes matters, separates them from material conditions, but is just as cosmotic as Dante. For Plato, too, what is is as it should be.

In contrast to these two predecessor descents, which depict Justice as cosmic and the cosmos as just, *The Descent of Alette* presents the order of things as something to be contended against. Like Dante's hell, Notley's subway is populated with monstrosities. For example, in the first ten pages alone, we are told that on the subway in which Alette finds herself: < "There are animals"... "But they" // "are mute & sad" >; < "There are corpses" >; there is a woman with < "...a misshapen" "slowing foot..." >; there are men with animal heads; there is an animal-mother with large, furry forearms, who is < "a long-haired, large cat" >; there is a mother and child who are < "...both on fire, continuously" > with a fire that is contained in them, and who are accompanied by < "The / ghost" "of the father" "[sitting] in flames" "beside them" >; and there is a car in which each passenger is encased by a colorless gray ghost, each encasing identical to the next.

*Un*like Dante, though, the monstrosities in *Alette* do not realize the enforcement of Justice, but take place in its absence, even *as* its absence. For example, in one section Alette reports having < "approached" "a large cavern" "above the door of which" "was / written" ("carved in rock") "the words *Mother Ship*" >. Alette enters the cavern and finds a clipper ship with its sails folded. It proves no "normal" ship, though, but one monstrous enough that Alette wonders whether the ship is someone's head. She enters, and invokes the Mother: < "I call on you" "to speak to me" >. In response to her invocation, the monster-ship slowly becomes animated. She (the monster-ship, or the Mother who possesses and is possessed by it) has difficulty speaking, managing only a low wheeze, but in that wheeze declares that her < "...real voice" "is further" "further down, in" // "another place" >, toward which she beckons Alette, urging her to keep walking. But no release or redemption occurs. The doors and windows just return from their soft, animated state to hard and static, and the house is decrepit: dirty, empty of furniture, inhabited by ants crawling on the floor. No cosmic justice is embodied in the ship and its monstrosity, and no enlightenment, no Dantesque moral, is offered Alette or the reader by encountering the ship. Alette concludes only with the report that < "It made me sad," "it made me sad" "I walked out / slowly" >, after which we never see the ship or hear its voice again.

Even sections identified by their placement as particularly important do not offer the kind of cosmic consonance Dante so consistently details.

As Alette crosses a river from one part of the underworld to the next, in the first section of Book Three, swimming < "in a moonless," "starless darkness" > and breathing fresh, sweet river air, monstrosity occurs again: < "the others I contained —" "my companions / from the subway —" "weightlessly" "emerged from me," "looking / shadow-like," > and with solid bodies began to swim with her. This placidity and concord is broken by another emergence from within Alette: < "something else, a substance," "a state of being," / "a thick noxious" "distress" "in the form of" "a gray cloud," // "welled up within me" "& left my body" >. The cloud proves to be full of < "ghoulish faces," "phosphorescent" "death's / heads;" >, one of which screams at Alette that < "'We are dying" "You are killing us" "killing us'" >. After this accusation, the cloud explodes into green flames that are then consumed by the darkness. But as with the Mother Ship, though, no reason for the suffering of the death's heads is offered, no resolution is offered, no cosmic Justice is manifest in the situation. Nothing comes of the encounter. Alette reports only that < "We turned over" "& resumed" "our swimming" >. The reader never again hears the voice of the glowing-haired death's head.

Like Plato's cave, Notley's subway is a < "world of souls" >. But Notley's underground is not merely the shadowy counter to the real world, a hypothetical figure for deprivation of agency and acuity. It is more complex than Plato's underground, more ambiguously related to reality. Alette reports in one section having entered < "a dark cavern" "that had a marked-off" "rear area" / "a little like" "a stage" >, in which she saw < "strange / figures" "dim figures" "in that space" "Like moving" "gray line / drawings" >. So far, so Platonic. But the Plato-like-ness doesn't last. Soon a man who entered the mysterious space emerges from it reporting that he dreamed he was not a body but < "a drinking vessel" "of red" / "cut glass" "with figures" "carved around me:" >. He reports that someone filled him with water and drank from him and that < "The glass could" "taste the water'" >. Unlike Plato's anonymous shades, none with individuality or identity or critical intelligence until it is given them by the philosopher who returns to the cave from his visit to the light above, Notley's "dim figures" are individuals, with individual histories and identities, and individual responses to individual experiences. Unlike Plato's cave, in which any individual agency must be brought to the shades from outside, in Notley's cave the shades retain agency.

From that "dark cavern" with its strange, dim, gray-line-drawing-like figures, Alette goes immediately to another, < "a cavern" "crowded with" "shadowy people" >, where she stands feeling drowsy and thinking to herself she is asleep even though she is functioning as if she were awake. Again, though, Alette first sees the group, but then encounters one person who emerges from the group. In this cavern (which, unlike Plato's, has material presence, not only conceptual presence: it has a dirty floor crawling with brown bugs), in place of the man with the drinking-vessel dream, < "A gray-haired woman," "lank-haired / chipmunk-jowled," "speaking to herself, came" "towards me —" >. Like the dream-reporting man, the chipmunk-jowled woman is a particular person, with particular characteristics: < "she smelled of urine—" >. In this case, though, it is Alette, not the person she encounters, who seems to be dreaming. After she hands the woman < "a sickly" "greenish orchid," "yellow-green" "that looked like / plastic" >, the woman simply vanishes, leaving Alette among a "crowd of others" in that cavern which has already been established as her own house and her own bed. But the visit to the cave ends with an anticlimax: < "Then I left the cave —" "& woke up," "seemed to wake up" / "as if I had" "been dreaming" >.

Plato's cave operates allegorically, within a clear and legible value system determined by the correlation of light with truth and darkness with error, and thus is susceptible to straightforward explication: "...if you interpret the upward journey of the soul [out of the cave] to the intelligible realm, you'll grasp what I hope to convey," namely that the form of the good "is the cause of all that is correct and beautiful in anything, that it produces both light and its source in the visible realm, and that in the intelligible realm it controls and provides truth and understanding, so that anyone who is to act sensibly in private or public must see it." In Plato's world, things are as they ought to be, so any discord between myself and how things are is my own failure, and my project is to adapt myself to how things are. Notley's underground is differently situated, in a world that is not as it should be, so Alette's project is not to fix herself, making sure she is like the already-perfect world, but to fix the world, which is profoundly flawed.

Dante's descent and Plato's descent both are quests of attunement, the goal of which is consonance with what is. They are cosmotic, unconditionally affirming what is. Notley's descent, though, is a quest of defiance, a rejection of and a battle *against* what is, a fight to defeat the tyrant. *The Descent of Alette*, then, is to the *Republic* and the *Inferno* as the Book of Job is to Deuteronomy. The "Deuteronomic theology" holds that reward attends virtue. If I am good (if I do as God commands), then I am rewarded; if I am bad, I am punished. Job, though, questions that correlation. Job's complaint is that he is a counterexample: he has been good, but punishment rather than reward has followed. In Deuteronomy, ultimately things *are* as they *ought to be*; not so in Job. Job must contend with God. Similarly, in Plato and Dante, ultimately things are as they ought to be, but not so in Notley. And *that* is what I mean by speaking of *The Descent of Alette* in terms of dissent: not that it names particular political failures or protests specific historical decisions, but that it denies the conceptual framework within which alone it could make sense to identify nation with Justice. A poetry of consent affirms, and a poetry of dissent denies, the cosmotism that conditions patriotism. In contrast to two of its famous predecessor descents, the *Inferno* and the allegory of the cave, both of which are poems of consent, affirmations of cosmotism, *The Descent of Alette* is a poem of dissent, one that takes Justice not as a cosmic fact guaranteeing that justice is always already in place, but as a still-distant ideal that orients and politicizes our obligations and labors, an ideal that may be realized only by struggle, by *contesting* the way things are, defying "the sons-of-bitches in Washington and Wall Street and L.A.," killing the tyrant.

Article 6:
Ask me once, stranger you; ask me twice, stranger me.

6.1: Poetry For Xenophilia

By *strangers* we often refer to persons previously unknown to ourselves. But in her title, *The Vertical Interrogation of Strangers*, Bhanu Kapil, a poet of Indian ancestry, born in England, currently living in the U.S., uses the word in a way that includes but also extends beyond that common meaning, an extension we may elucidate by contrasting it to a prior literary usage, that of Albert Camus, a writer of partly Spanish ancestry, born in Algiers, living at the time of his most famous works in France. Camus's stranger discloses his character in such self-reports as his noting that, just before he and his friends encountered "the Arabs" with whom he had a conflict, "I wasn't thinking about anything, because I was half asleep from the sun beating down on my bare head." He is a stranger not because others do not know him but because he is alienated from his own experience.

Camus's stranger undergoes interrogation by the authorities, but even in the preceding "friendly" interrogation the stranger finds it hard "to tell [his own lawyer] what he wanted to know." Nor is the stranger able to satisfy other interrogators. After his first meeting with the magistrate, the stranger says, "I got the impression he didn't understand." His estrangement in relation to other people derives from his estrangement from himself, itself a function of estrangement from his current circumstances. So far, the same might be said of the strangers Kapil interrogates. But there is a twist. Camus's stranger merits an honorific, "the absurd hero," because his estrangement appears, to the colonizing males to whom Camus addresses his story, elected rather than imposed: society entitles him to his experience, and expels him only after he has elected estrangement.

Kapil's strangers are offered no such entitlement. Meursault makes himself a stranger; society makes Kapil's subjects strangers. Her subjects are strangers Kapil "met in theaters, forests, laundromats, temples and diners," and who spoke (as if to make a virtue of necessity) on condition of anonymity. Kapil describes her research: "From January 12, 1992, to June 4, 1996, I traveled in India, England, and the United States, interviewing Indian women of diverse ages and backgrounds." Kapil asked her subjects to respond "to one or more of a predetermined selection of twelve questions," within a time limit of thirty minutes, during which "the questionee was locked in a room without windows, furniture, or overhead lighting." Kapil reports that she sought "an honest and swift text, uncensored by guilt or the desire to construct an impressive, publishable 'finish.'" During the period when she was conducting the interviews, Kapil "answered the questions for myself again and again," recording her responses "in a notebook, on scraps," and "on stickers that I affixed to escalator tubing, café tables, shop windows."

Kapil's method of preparing for, and engaging in, the act of writing poetry (sited, as it is, far from "emotion recollected in tranquility") implicitly reassesses any standard of valuation that awards inherent validity to the writing of the colonizers and withholds it from the writing of the colonized.

Kapil's method of writing, which she describes as "editing" an "anthology" of responses by persons whose voices are not often recorded, does not enact familiar notions of inspiration or self-expression, but it does accord with Salman Rushdie's take, in the title essay of *Imaginary Homelands*, on the sense of estrangement he considers characteristic of the situation of Indians abroad. "[I]t's my present," Rushdie says, "that is foreign, and... the past is home, albeit a lost home in a lost city in the mists of lost time." That discrepant temporality makes inevitable a sense of loss, "some urge to reclaim, to look back, even at the risk of being mutated into pillars of salt." But looking back only "gives rise to profound uncertainties," because "physical alienation from India almost inevitably means that we will not be capable of reclaiming precisely the thing that was lost; that we will, in short, create fictions, not actual cities or villages, but invisible ones, imaginary homelands, Indias of the mind." The pattern (discrepant temporality, loss, confinement to an imaginary that substitutes for an inaccessible reality rather than supplementing a present reality) continues; next follows fragmentation. "[W]hen the Indian writer who writes from outside India tries to reflect that world, he is obliged to deal in broken mirrors," but, Rushdie points out, the fragments, paradoxically, may be more valuable than the intact mirror. "The shards of memory acquired greater status, greater resonance, because they were *remains*; fragmentation made trivial things seem like symbols, and the mundane acquired numinous qualities."

Fragmentation brings with it partiality. Because humans are unable to "perceive things whole," because "we are not gods but wounded creatures, cracked lenses, capable only of fractured perceptions," writers "are no longer sages, dispensing the wisdom of the centuries," and writers "who have been forced by cultural displacement to accept the provisional nature of all truths, all certainties," in their estrangement from Olympus are "released to describe our worlds in the way in which all of us, whether writers or not, perceive it from day to day." Rushdie's word "provisional" seems key. An interrogator alert to "the provisional nature of all truths" will be alert also to any truths the stranger being interrogated wishes to provide.

The English word for fear of, and hostility toward, strangers, *xenophobia*, derives from the Greek word *xenos*. But the range of meaning for the Greek *xenos* differs from that for the English *stranger*. Liddell and Scott give *hospes* as the Latin equivalent, and report that *xenos* meant first "*the friend*, with whom one has a treaty of hospitality: in this sense both parties are *xenos*, and the relation was hereditary." In other words, though the foregrounded characteristic in *stranger* is lack of affiliation, in *xenos* the foregrounded characteristic is affiliation. Liddell and Scott enumerate other meanings: "in Homer mostly *the guest*, as opp. to *the host*," "any *stranger*, as being entitled to the rights of hospitality," "a common term of address" (*o xene, O stranger*), etc.

"Vertical interrogation" posits xeno*philia* in place of xeno*phobia*, by assuming an inherited treaty of hospitality. Vertical interrogation returns the stranger to her original status as holder of rights, locus of honor. Vertical interrogation of a stranger accords her not the "absurd hero" status of Meursault nor the "enemy combatant" vilification imputed to the strangers interrogated at Guantánamo and Abu Ghraib, but the status accorded to Odysseus in the palace of Demodokos, status as one whose story is asked for and then wept over.

How one construes "stranger" and how one practices "interrogation" are not unrelated, as the U.S. has demonstrated in its foreign policy since 9/11. The Executive Order issued on 20 July 2007 by President George W. Bush is representative. It names, as if it were a single polity, "al Qaeda, the Taliban, and associated forces," and reaffirms a prior "determination" (from 7 February 2002) that members of this purported polity are "unlawful enemy combatants" and therefore "not entitled to the protections that the Third Geneva Convention provides to prisoners of war." The construction of stranger sets the terms of the interrogation: I determine whether you are a stranger; association with "bad guys" is adequate grounds for such a determination; your status as stranger appoints me the interrogator, awards me all rights, and denies you any rights. That you as a stranger know nothing of value to me except information that might help me thwart the threat to me that I say you pose preempts reciprocity, removes any constraints on my mode of interrogation.

Kapil is not alone in wanting to embody an alternative to the ways of relating interrogation to strangers depicted by Camus and enacted in U.S. foreign policy. In *Letters from Abu Ghraib*, Joshua Casteel, a U.S. military interrogator who eventually became a conscientious objector, records his search, if not for *vertical* interrogation of strangers, then for *upright* interrogation. Early in the book, Casteel seeks to alter the relationship of interrogation to stranger, even without questioning the aims of interrogation imposed by his military superiors. He asserts that an alternative view of the stranger and correlative revision of practices of interrogation achieves those aims more fully. He believes that "no one actually wants secrecy, to carry the memory of shameful actions alone," and therefore an "aggressive approach" to interrogation encourages the interrogated to go against those useful-to-the-interrogator desires, but "a relationship of understanding" successfully uses "a person's internal belief scheme to encourage them to narrate dishonorable actions with their own words." Eventually he rejects the aims of interrogation imposed on him. Aims that exclude consideration of the well-being of the stranger are incompatible with upright interrogation. "I have simply lacked the ability," he says in his application for conscientious objector status, "to look at the person I interrogate in a way that does not demand I also think about what is best for him," which makes his dilemma less "of moral action" than "of sheer IDENTITY."

Kapil's § 72 begins with an interrogation of the speaker *as* a stranger. "I am not writing about myself as a rational human being. I am writing about the substances of an animal and female life: magic, pain, the cracked nails of four feet, and the days like this one...." Attempts to evaluate poetry tend to assume what is implicit in Dana Gioia's question, "Can poetry matter?," namely that the value of poetry will inhere in what poetry accomplishes, in its use value. Here I insinuate an alternative, that more of poetry's value lies in what is than in what it does, more in its intrinsic value than in its use value. Bhanu Kapil's *The Vertical Interrogation of Strangers*, published in 2001, must have been written before 9/11 and before the public disclosures of torture in U.S. detention facilities. Subsequent U.S. policy decisions demonstrate that the book did not have discernible political effects. Kapil's book makes nothing happen. But one value of poetry is not its political *effects* but its political *implications*. Poetry, whether or not it *accomplishes* anything, is akin to civil disobedience in positing, and embracing, an alternative ideal. Poetry recognizes strangers, and interrogates them, in fulfillment of such recognition, vertically.

6.2: Poetry For Change

Between Bhanu Kapil's *The Vertical Interrogation of Strangers* and Jacqueline Jones LaMon's *Last Seen* there occurs a *turn*. In structuring *Last Seen*, her collection of poems "inspired by actual case histories of long-term missing African American children," LaMon opens with a section called "Polygraph: The Control Questions," and ends with a section called "Polygraph: The Guilty Knowledge Test." The two sections contain six poems each, and each of those twelve poems bears as its title a question (e.g., "Who are you and whom do you love?"). The questions, though, do not come from the case histories that give the book its subject, nor from the protocol for polygraph testing in law enforcement. Nor did LaMon make up the questions herself. Instead, they come from *The Vertical Interrogation of Strangers*.

The questions, identified in Kapil's book simply as "Twelve Questions," are listed there on their own page after the "Introduction" and before the first poem. They are:

1. Who are you and whom do you love?
2. Where did you come from / how did you arrive?
3. How will you begin?
4. How will you live now?
5. What is the shape of your body?
6. Who was responsible for the suffering of your mother?
7. What do you remember about the earth?
8. What are the consequences of silence?

9. Tell me what you know about dismemberment.

10. Describe a morning you woke without fear.

11. How will you / have you prepare(d) for your death?

12. And what would you say if you could?

In *The Vertical Interrogation of Strangers*, each question is posed repeatedly: each of the 98 sections in the book employs one of the questions as its title.

Kapil says nothing of her reasons for posing the questions. She only gives the circumstances ("From January 12, 1992, to June 4, 1996, I traveled in India, England, and the United States, interviewing women of diverse ages and backgrounds"), and contrasts her expectations ("— The project as I thought it would be: an anthology of the voices of Indian women") to the results ("— The project as I wrote it: a tilted plane"). LaMon, though, in her "Note" acknowledging her appropriation of the questions, imputes to Kapil a purpose that Kapil herself did not state; LaMon asserts that Kapil "posed her questions to women of Indian descent to find a way to freedom and peace." LaMon affirms that purpose by adapting and extending it: "I believe these questions should be answered in truth by every woman at least once during the course of her life." By re-presenting and adapting the questions in *Last Seen*, LaMon gives a turn to *The Vertical Interrogation of Strangers*.

The suggestion is not primarily an evaluative gesture but an interrogative one. It happens that I appreciate the quality in Kapil's work that invites a reader to take the questions as posed to her/him, and that I also appreciate the kind of active reading/writing merger that LaMon practices through this appropriation, but I seek here, not to persuade others toward my esteem for these books, only to raise questions about the turn. In reflection toward this essay, I found that my own prototype of the turn assumed that the turn takes place within a single poem. Taking that feature for granted, though, narrows one's understanding of the turn, and therefore, to some meaningful degree, distorts one's understanding of poetry. Noting an example that does *not* have that feature raises questions about the implications of taking it for granted. As a respectful bow toward Kapil's questions and LaMon's appropriation of them, it seems fitting to make the following list twelve questions long.

1. Does a turn always and only happen *in* a poem, or can a turn happen *to* a poem?

2. What is turned by a turn? Is the turning effected by a turn transitive or intransitive?

3. Who may effect a turn? Only the "original" poet?

4. Is the turn an *element* of the poem's *structure*, or can it (also) be an *event* in the *relationship* between poet and poem and reader? Is the turn an *architectural* feature, or an *ecological* feature?

5. *Where* does the turn happen? Within the poem? Within the reader? Among the community of readers? Across a poem's history?

6. Does applying "turn" to such a case *extend* the concept of turn, or merely pervert it?

7. How must the roles of writer and reader shift in order to accommodate this as an example of a turn?

8. If the possibility that a turn may occur after a poem is published bears analogy to Aristotle's claim that a person seemingly happy in life may become unhappy after death, what is the concept analogous to Aristotle's *eudaimonia* that is being modified?

9. Would an understanding of the turn that accommodated this example make our understanding of poetry more performative (place the "poem itself" in the reading of it as the "song itself" is, we might say, in the performance more than in the score), or would it give the *text* even more emphasis than we place on it already?

10. Would we consider it relevant if we learned that Kapil and LaMon also thought of this example as a turn? If we learned that either or both of them *rejected* thinking of it in this way?

11. If a turn can be given one poet's work by another poet ten years later, have the boundaries of the individual poem been breached or blurred (as, say, the boundaries of the individual organism are blurred by symbiotic understandings in biology)?

12. How must we think of a *poem* if we accept this example as an example of the turn?

In thinking about and speaking of the "turn" in poetry, it is easy to forget that the term is a metaphor, and that its vehicle (directionality) is not its tenor (change). The turn enacts or marks a change, though that change is only metaphorically a change of direction. I take it that *Last Seen*, by such differences as recontextualizing the questions, dividing them into two groups, and orienting them toward a stated purpose, has created change to *The Vertical Interrogation of Strangers*. Applying to that change the metaphor of the turn occasions inquiry in two directions: toward illuminating the poems by thinking of their relationship as realizing a turn, and toward illuminating the turn by considering as one example what happens between *The Vertical Interrogation of Strangers* and *Last Seen*.

Article 7:
No secrets means no exceptions.

7.1: Poetry Against Expectations

If a reader remembers anything from Emily Dickinson's 258 precisely, word for word, it is likely to be the first two lines, "There's a certain Slant of light, / Winter Afternoons —." If a reader remembers anything from Heather McHugh's "What He Thought" precisely, word for word, it is likely to be the *last* two lines, "poetry is what // he thought, but did not say." Accounting for that experiential difference would suggest insights into poetic craft. Here I focus on placement of the "synoptic moment," by which I mean the poem's point of gestalt, when the reader's attention is broadest, most "big picture." I mean, in other words, the moment of epiphany or dramatic resolution, the point at which the whole is implicit in the part. Dickinson's "There's a certain Slant of light" represents a pattern of disclosure I'll call *expository*: the synoptic moment occurs first thing (in those memorable first two lines), and the rest of the poem explicates it. McHugh's "What He Thought" represents the contrary pattern, which I'll call *cumulative*: it gives clues along the way, but does not offer up the synoptic moment until the end (in those memorable last two lines).

Placement of the synoptic moment (its location in or distribution through the poem) operates as one element of craft. *Any* poem (any literary work, in fact, in any genre) must manage its means of disclosure, and noting these two patterns, expository and cumulative, as the ends of a continuum will help me decide how to manage disclosure: give the synoptic moment early and explore it, or drop clues all along but withhold the synoptic moment until the end, or take some middle way. By focusing here on the *ends* of the continuum, I seek to open the *whole* continuum.

By "craft" I mean here having answered, through the writing of it, two questions about a poem: 1. *What are this poem's aims?* 2. *What must I do to enable the poem to fulfill its aims?* (I mean, that is, to include *both* of what are distinguished in 1.2 above as "craft" and "metacraft.") The first question, *What are this poem's aims?*, matters because poetry's powers are extensive and various. Unless I *choose* a poem's aims, I remain confined to received aims, those most typical of my time and place. As in other areas of life, so in poetry: until I identify my own ambition, I merely fulfill the expectations of others, confirming and replicating what Lauren Berlant calls the "metastructure of consent." We get accustomed nowadays to what Adrienne Rich calls "the columnar, anecdotal, domestic poem," but nothing confines us to that formula. Homer composed poems that chronicled the war and the homecoming that gave the Greeks a national identity, and Dante wrote a poem that tried to synthesize all the cosmological and spiritual knowledge of his age. It wasn't just his own religious experience Milton sought to explore in *Paradise Lost*: he set out to "justify the ways of God to men."

Deliberate choice of aims by no means excludes anecdotal domestic poems: I may still savor how I felt that morning by the shore as I sipped my steaming coffee and watched the sun rise over the sea. That's a valid aim; it's just not the only one available to me. *Choosing* my aim opens other possibilities as well: I might express my bliss over a morning of leisure in a comfortable and beautiful setting, or I might decide, as does C. D. Wright in *One Big Self*, to overcome "the resistance of poetry to the conventions of evidentiary writing," and to speak with prisoners in three Louisiana prisons, toward the aim of reuniting "the separated with the larger human enterprise." I might decide, as does Nathaniel Mackey in *Splay Anthem*, to reinterpret the Dogon myth of the Andoumboulou, "as not simply a failed or flawed, earlier form of human being but a rough draft of human being, the work-in-progress we continue to be," doing so in fulfillment of a not-exclusively-personal aspiration toward a less flawed humanity. Or, again, I might decide, as does Bhanu Kapil in *The Vertical Interrogation of Strangers*, to spend four years travelling "in India, England, and the United States, interviewing Indian women of diverse ages and backgrounds," as preparation for a description of my own body that will "tilt" an anthology of others' voices.

Craft is not free-floating; it's anchored to aim. The same word choices that would make a poem well crafted if I want you to laugh would make it badly crafted if I want you to cry. And craft is anchored to aim for the same reason that, say, travel is. MapQuest can't give me directions unless I tell it where I'm going. Is it a better decision, when I'm entering I-80, to take the eastbound on-ramp or the westbound one? Depends on whether I'm headed to Portland, Oregon, or to Portland, Maine. Similarly, the quality of the craft in a word choice or sentence construction is conditional rather than absolute: good if it furthers the poem's aim, bad if not. It is part of craft to ask the poem's aims: where is this poem, or ought it be, headed?

The second question of craft, *What must I do to enable the poem to fulfill its aims?*, matters because craft occurs as a series of *decisions*. Once I've told it where I am and where I'm going, MapQuest gives me an abbreviated decision tree. Should I turn right or left at the end of my block? Turn right. Etc. (Abbreviated in that it leaves most decisions unstated. It tells me to turn left on 26th, and leaves me to infer a bunch of other advice: Should I turn left on 21st? No. Should I turn left on 22nd? No...) Craft in writing, too, realizes a decision tree: it's far more complicated than MapQuest directions, so many decisions get made subconsciously. If MapQuest has to leave many decisions to the driver's contextual understanding and driving competence, so must the writing process allow the writer's competence to manage many of the steps in the decision tree. Still, it's important to recognize that when we write we're *making decisions*, and a lot of them.

Failing to ask after the poem's aims inclines a poet unreflectively to accept the anecdotal domestic poem as the only possibility; failing to ask how to fulfill those aims is to pretend writing results from inspiration. If it did, then creative writing programs would deserve the opprobrium frequently heaped on them. MFA faculty would be perpetrators, and MFA students victims, of a scam. Inspiration can't be taught. I have no influence over the caprice of the muses or the favor of the gods, and I can't help anyone else gain such influence. It *is* possible, at least in principle, to help one another make better decisions (including the subconscious ones). Since craft results from a series of decisions, attention to the decision process is important. When I tried to learn to play classical guitar, my teacher had to remind me that practicing a piece *often* wouldn't help me play it *better*, if I was practicing it *wrongly*. Practicing a piece often but wrongly would only ensure that I install mistakes and infelicities securely into muscle memory. Same here. We can practice decision-making, but without reflection on the decision-making process itself, we're just *ingraining* our decision-making habits rather than *refining* them. *How* we decide matters.

Craft results from purposive decision-making. *How* we make decisions in writing a poem will influence how good those decisions are. One helpful decision-making process is to regard various aspects of a poem and its construction as occurring along continua, each continuum defined by an opposition. One such aspect is the disclosure of key information (and perspective, and tone, etc.) in the poem. This continuum is defined by two poles: analytic development after early synopsis, and synthetic development toward late synopsis. Emily Dickinson's 258 stands near the early synopsis extreme, Heather McHugh's "What He Thought" near the late synopsis extreme.

By calling the Dickinson poem "expository" I only mean that the controlling image is given at the start ("There's a certain Slant of light, / Winter Afternoons —"), after which the poem explicates that image, drawing out its implications and significance. The first two lines could stand alone as their own poem: "There's a certain Slant of light, / Winter Afternoons —" sounds compact and complete, like Ezra Pound's two-line poem, "In a Station of the Metro." No other couplet in Dickinson's poem, though, stands alone in that way: each later couplet depends on the first. For instance, "When it comes, the Landscape listens— / Shadows— hold their breath—" depends grammatically on the first couplet: the "it" needs a referent, the slant of light. Dickinson could have left off the last stanza, which continues the process of explication, but not the first, which gives the subject to be explicated.

Dickinson first shows the slant of light, then enumerates its qualities. What does the slant of light do? It oppresses us. How does it do so? Just the way hymns in church do. What is its effect on us? Heavenly Hurt, that paradoxical combination of suffering and ecstasy that devotional poetry has recorded for us again and again. Recall, for instance, the biblical Psalm 13, which opens with "How long, O Lord? Will you forget me forever?" and ends only a few lines later with "I will sing to the Lord, / because he has dealt bountifully with me." Or John Donne's ecstatic request, "Batter my heart, three-personed God; /... / Except you enthrall me, never shall be free, / Nor ever chaste, except you ravish me." Or Hopkins' sonnets. Even Anne Carson's plea, muffled by the second person: "The kind of sadness that is a black suction pipe extracting you / from your own navel and which the Buddhists call // 'no mindcover' is a sign of God." How does the slant of light change us? Not physically, but spiritually. It does not leave a physical trace, a scar, but instead wounds internally. Why internally? Because inside us is "Where the Meanings, are—." How do we come to know the slant of light? Only by immediate experience of it, not by being told about it. With what emotional state is it identified? Not bliss or joy, but despair. Does it affect only us? No, the whole world participates in the experience; the landscape, and the shadows in it, experience it just as we do. What part of the human cycle does it anticipate? Death.

The expository poem reviews, looks backward in time. Though the Dickinson poem contains an implicit notice about the future (there will be a certain slant of light on future winter afternoons), it gets to that notice by still implicit but even more basic attention to a past instance (there was a certain slant of light one winter afternoon). In structure, an expository poem resembles a fugue, or an opera. In a fugue, the theme is stated as the beginning of the piece, and development of the theme (through various permutations and repetitions) constitutes the piece. In opera, the overture introduces the listener at the beginning to themes that will be developed more fully through the larger work that follows. In Dickinson, the "certain slant of light" is developed as an oppressive slant, a wounding slant, a transformative slant, a despair-inducing slant, a premonitory slant, and so on. An expository poem invites the reader to stillness. Our proxy, the imagined self that joins the speaker in the room on that winter afternoon, does not move during the poem, but stays still and looks and contemplates. A visual correlative of an expository poem, then, would be a painting, which invites one to stand before it. An expository poem will tend to be meditative, static, cerebral, analytical. Its "action" will occur inside the reader, as thought.

Of course there are countless other examples of expository poems. Wallace Stevens' "The Snow Man," for example, delivers what Kant calls a hypothetical imperative. "One must have a mind of winter," the speaker tells us, but that obligation is not categorical. One must have a mind of winter *if* one wants to "regard the frost" and "behold the junipers shagged with ice," and so on. The imperative is the synoptic moment, the part that contains the whole, but the exposition of the imperative (in this case through qualification of it) then occupies the rest of the poem.

The synoptic moment in an expository poem need not even be *in* the poem. For James Wright's short poem "From a Bus Window in Central Ohio, Just Before a Thunder Shower," the *title* is the synoptic moment, and the poem the exposition: if you were in a bus riding through central Ohio, the poem says, you would see "cribs loaded with roughage [huddling] to-gether," and so on. Nor is the expository structure limited to short lyric poems. *The Iliad*, for example, a long narrative poem in twenty-four books that total over 15,000 lines, begins with a synopsis in its first lines, even in its first *word*. The first line might be translated "Sing, goddess, the rage of Achilles the son of Peleus," but that capitulation to English grammar misses the fact that in Greek the sentence begins with *menis*, the word for rage, a feature Robert Fagles captures by cheating a little and repeating the word: "Rage — Goddess, sing the rage of Peleus' son Achilles."

The expository mode risks didacticism and tedium. Didacticism is easy to see with a little time and intellectual distance. Oliver Wendell Holmes's "The Chambered Nautilus," for instance, uses the expository mode, begin-ning with "This is the ship of pearl," and then expatiating on the shell of the chambered nautilus at some length, but the last stanza, which communi-cates the "heavenly message" brought by the shell, sounds like it belongs on a "Successories" motivational print:

> Build thee more stately mansions, O my soul,
> As the swift seasons roll!
> Leave thy low-vaulted past!
> Let each new temple, nobler than the last,
> Shut thee from heaven with a dome more vast,
> Till thou at length art free,
> Leaving thine outgrown shell by life's unresting sea!

Holmes has taken the easiest path, using the "exposition" to interpret the ex-perience of seeing the shell so that it fulfills the expectations of his society. Any act of interpretation will be tempted to normalize the object of interpre-tation in this way, so expository poems, in which the mode of disclosure is interpretive, will need, in the words of Sherod Santos, "to push beyond those elements we *already recognize*, those elements that normally serve as both the end and limit of our knowing." Dickinson fulfills that responsibility; Holmes does not. Which helps demonstrate why craft decisions have to do with form *and* content. Just as it is easy to accept received generic limitations — to write only anecdotal domestic poems — without even realizing it, so is it easy in one's poems to stay safely within the domain of what we already recognize.

In Heather McHugh's "What He Thought," at least two related things happen: an historical event is recounted, and the speaker undergoes a personal transformation, from glibness to gravity. But both happen within a narrative context which must be laid out, so both the recounting of the historical event and the transformation occur later in the poem, *after* the establishment of the context. The recounting of the historical event and the personal transformation merge in the synoptic moment, which arrives only at the very end of the poem.

The speaker tells of "do[ing] a job in Italy" as one of a small group of "Poets from America." They are hosted cordially, but they stick to their various roles, as "the academic, the apologist, / the arrogant, the amorous, / the brazen and the glib." The speaker is dismissive of the Italian host, whose poetry she can't access because she doesn't read Italian, and whose "suit / of regulation gray" leads her to regard him as an "administrator" and a "conservative." On the last evening of the visit, though, as they "chatted" in the "family restaurant" chosen by the host, one of the "Poets from America," trying to "be poetic," asks, "What's poetry? / Is it the fruits and vegetables and / marketplace of Campo dei Fiori, or / the statue there?" The speaker blurts out the glib answer that it's both, but the "underestimated host" speaks out "all of a sudden, with a rising passion," about the meaning of the statue, that it "represents Giordano Bruno, / brought to be burned in the public square / because of his offense against / authority." The host recounts the grisly public burning, reporting that "That is how / [Bruno] died: without a word, in front / of everyone," and concluding with an answer to the question "What is poetry?" that is more resonant than the speaker's glib answer. Poetry, the host opines, in a soft voice and after a dramatic pause, "is what // [Bruno] thought, but did not say." By calling this poem "cumulative" I mean to note that it offers us context, situation, and conflict gradually, building toward the key point, the "clincher" (what I am calling the "synoptic moment"), which it saves for those last two lines. The pieces of the puzzle add up slowly. The title includes the pronoun "he," but we don't know until line 69 (the last line of the poem) who the "he" of the title is. Indeed, one structural feature at work in the poem is the ambiguous reference. I take it that "he" refers to both Giordano Bruno and "our underestimated host," suggesting that the thoughts of both are important. The first word of the poem is "we," but we the readers don't learn until the fourth line that the "we" in the poem refers to a group of poets from America. Introduction to the other characters is also delayed. The Italian host does not appear until line 14 (and doesn't speak for himself until thirty lines later), and Giordano Bruno does not appear until line 45.

If in the Dickinson poem we stand still with the speaker, in the McHugh poem we move with the speaker through the events. Thus sculpture seems more apt than painting as an analogue from the visual arts. A painting invites one to stand still in front of it, but a sculpture invites one to *move*. (So paintings are typically hung on a wall, sculptures placed outdoors or in the middle of a room, so that viewers may walk around them.) Even if the invitation to move around a sculpture is implicit, it still is present, as in the pedimental sculptures from the Parthenon, which, though they were to be mounted in such a way that only the front would be seen, nonetheless were finished also in the back. In Dickinson, we stay in one room for the whole poem. In McHugh, we fly to Italy, are driven from Rome to Fano, go sightseeing, visit the speaker's pensione room, go to a restaurant, visit the Campo dei Fiori, and return to the year 1600 for the execution of a heretic.

An expository poem invites the reader to stillness; a cumulative poem, to movement. Expository poems tend toward the meditative, static, cerebral, and analytical; cumulative poems, toward the suspenseful, dynamic, visceral, and synthetic. Ideas get presented in the McHugh poem (which, after all, is about what he *thought*), but it's not *intellectual* sympathy we come to feel for Bruno. We don't first identify with his ideas, and therefore feel that he shouldn't die; we identify with his persecution, the injustice of which inclines us toward receptivity to his ideas.

If the basic gesture of an expository poem is to review, to look backward in time, the basic gesture of a cumulative poem is to foreshadow, to look forward in time. In "What He Thought," the first four words, "We were supposed to," create expectation. Similarly, at lines 41-2, we are told that "What followed / taught me something about difficulty," from which we know to anticipate that we will soon see what followed, and that we ourselves also will learn something about difficulty. To the very end of the poem, the pattern of withholding information and creating anticipation continues. The host has been speaking "with a rising passion" for twenty lines, but just as he is about to deliver the punch line, the speaker of the poem interrupts to tell us that "we'd all put down our forks by now, to listen," a delay that heightens the already high tension in the poem. That the host speaks "with a rising passion" works like a stage direction to suggest that for cumulative poems the most apt musical analogy is the crescendo: the tension builds as it does through long passages in, say, "Bolero" or Beethoven's 9th or Gorecki's 3rd.

The expository mode threatens didacticism and tedium; the dangers of the cumulative mode are anticlimax and melodrama. "Casey at the Bat" exemplifies the latter. Information is meted out as necessary to build suspense and lead to the final synopsis. We learn in the first stanza that "the score stood two to four with just an inning left to play"; by the fourth stanza we've learned that the bases are loaded, with two out; by the tenth stanza, the count is 0-2 on mighty Casey. By the thirteenth and final stanza Casey has swung at the final pitch, but we learn from the poem's very last line that "there is no joy in Mudville — mighty Casey has struck out." The poem follows the cumulative mode of disclosure well enough, but it's melodramatic. The suspense is not justified by what is at stake in the action: it's a *game*, in *Mudville*.

Expository poems are easy to find, and so are cumulative poems. Sylvia Plath's "Daddy," for example, discloses information in a cumulative way. The title and the first word, "You," orient us to the poem's being an apostrophe by a child to her father, but from there things sum gradually to the conclusion. For example, the Nazi conceit is not introduced in its entirety and then explicated, but accumulates. In line 15, we get, out of the blue, the German words "Ach, du," and then enough description to let us know that Daddy was born into a German family in a town in Poland. In line 30, the German language is labelled "obscene," and the next stanza treats it as a shoah train "Chuffing me off like a Jew" to a concentration camp. In line 40, Daddy's Nazi affiliation becomes explicit: his preoccupation with the Luftwaffe and his "Aryan eye" are noted, and he is called "panzer-man." Then the speaker's husband is described as "a model" of the father: "A man in black with a Meinkampf look." To the Nazi characterization are added devils and vampires, until the culminating line, the synoptic moment, "Daddy, daddy, you bastard, I'm through."

Randall Jarrell's "Next Day" also adds up gradually to its synoptic moment. The speaker first places herself uneasily among the "food-gathering flocks" at the grocery store, but becomes increasingly self-reflective and increasingly troubled by "what I've become." She laments her loss of beauty, comparing her youth, when she was "good enough to eat," to today, when the boy helping her load her groceries in the car "doesn't see" her. We get information about her family (children away at school, husband away at work) and her "unvarying" routine, we see her looking at herself in the rear-view mirror, seeing "the eyes I hate, / The smile I hate," and then we learn (not until line 49) about "the funeral / I went to yesterday," the funeral of a friend who had once told her she looked young. The force of all this evidence accruing leads finally in the last line of the poem to the synoptic moment, the speaker's realization that her life "is commonplace and solitary."

I have concentrated on the extremes, the boundaries, in order to mark out a territory, but I should emphasize that the point here is that entire territory, not just those boundaries. To put this another way, though I have contrasted two extremes, my point is that we are *not* in an either/or situation in regard to disclosure. To *choose* between extremes presumes that there are only the extremes themselves; to *operate* between extremes presumes an area between the extremes. It is *not* that all poems follow one pattern or the other, but that most poems operate not *at* the extremes these poems exemplify, but *between* them. In this regard, my point is Aristotelian. Aristotle considers it a practical aid to virtue to identify the excess and defect in regard to passions and actions, because doing so allows us to choose the mean, which will reside between the excess and the defect. So for example, "With regard to feelings of fear and confidence courage is the mean," something we see in part because we see the extremes: the excess, rashness, and the defect, cowardice. Realizing the mean "is no easy task"; it is complicated by the fact that the extremes may not be equally contrary to the mean, and that I myself may incline more toward one extreme than the other, and so need to overcorrect. But the general pattern is clear. Similarly, it is a practical aid to craft to identify the extremes in regard to various aspects of the poem, because doing so allows us to choose where, along the continuum created, to place that aspect of our poem. Realizing craft is no easier than realizing virtue, but identifying extremes helps to clear a path toward craft.

7.2: Poetry Against Exceptionalism

Among persons attentive to contemporary global environmental concerns, the recent coinage "anthropocene" designates the newly manifest human capacity to alter the earth at a geological magnitude and time scale, including the possibility of altering the earth in such a way that it becomes uninhabitable for humanity itself. Toward theorizing an ethics and aesthetics adequate to that dangerous capacity (toward, that is, an eco-ethics and an eco-aesthetics), I note here one feature they share, namely a confluent resistance to exceptionalism. Though there may be various ways in which they *di*verge, eco-aesthetics and eco-ethics *con*verge in taking exception to exceptionalism.

The hegemony of exceptionalism in the discourses and institutions of contemporary society is indicated by the absence in our vocabulary of a term to name its opposite. That lexical void works to secure exceptionalism: our having *named* no alternative insinuates that there *is* no alternative. But that insinuation is wrong. There *is* an alternative to exceptionalism, so into the lexical void I cast the name *implicationalism*, declaring that both eco-aesthetics and eco-ethics urge implicationalism. The term is not a pretty one, but I coin it less for its beauty than for its etymological contrast to exceptionalism. "Exception" comes from the Latin prefix *ex-*, meaning "out of," and the Latin root *capere*, meaning "to take." To be an exception to something is to have been taken out of it. "Implication" comes from the Latin prefix *in-*, meaning "into, within, towards," and the Latin root *plicare*, meaning "to fold." To be implicated in something is to be folded into or within it. An exceptionalist view, then, exempts some x (a person, a nation, a species) from the rules or the circumstances that constrain others of its kind, by contrast to which an implicationalist view understands that x as folded, with others of its kind, into a shared context. Even four points of contrast, each gestured toward rather than exhaustively analyzed, should be enough to identify implicationalism *as* an alternative, and to invite further exploration of how eco-aesthetics and eco-ethics flow away from exceptionalism and toward implicationalism.

A first point would contrast concentration of agency with distribution of agency. Current human social structures result in high concentrations of agency. In a global economy organized as ours is, the rich get richer. In global politics that operates as ours does, the strong get stronger. Agency, in the form of its economic marker, money, or of its political correlative, power, gathers in piles, ever fewer and ever larger. Eco-ethics and eco-aesthetics, though, call for radical change, a total reorganization, in fulfillment of a different ideal, an increasingly even and broad distribution of agency (money, power, well-being), rather than the increasingly uneven and narrow distribution toward which contemporary global economic and political arrangements aim.

Capitalism tirelessly reinforces the premise that the collective welfare of humanity is the sum of the separate welfare of individual humans. The cultural analogue of this premise is that the collective expression of human culture is the sum of individual expressions of self. These premises sanction, and are sanctioned by, exceptionalism. Where summing is the question, any addition to my private welfare adds to the collective welfare: if *I* have more, then *we* have more. In contrast to these pervasive premises, eco-aesthetics and eco-ethics posit that the collective welfare of humanity is the *common* welfare, and the collective expression is the *common* expression. That is, eco-aesthetics and eco-ethics exemplify not exceptionalism but implicationalism. Instead of singling out the individual, making exception the ideal state, they embed the individual, emphasizing implication.

Capitalism allows for, even encourages, concentration of welfare (especially through its representative, wealth). I am invited to secure for myself as much as I am able to secure, on the grounds that any good I hold counts toward the collective good. Nothing does, and nothing should, limit my accumulation. There is no such thing as having too much, because *mine* always adds to *ours*. Eco-aesthetics and eco-ethics advocate the opposite: broader distribution of welfare, rather than more focused concentrations of it.

Andrew Carnegie gives a clear formulation of the exceptionalist logic of capitalism. Only two options, he claims, are open to humans: poverty for the many and wealth for a few, or poverty for all. Of those two, the former is preferable. Carnegie begins "The Gospel of Wealth" with a contrast between "former days," in which "there was little difference between the dwelling, dress, food, and environment of the chief and those of his retainers," and "our age," in which we enjoy a "highly beneficial" contrast "between the palace of the millionaire and the cottage of the laborer." Carnegie illustrates the bad option by recounting his "visiting the Sioux" (a lingering remnant, for him, of the primitive condition, in which the exceptional has not yet arisen) and being "led to the wigwam of the chief," which "was like the others in external appearance, and even within the difference was trifling between it and those of the poorest of his braves." The good option, on Carnegie's view, is the current state of affairs, in which the poorest still live in squalor but "the houses of some" are now "homes for all that is highest and best in literature and the arts, and for all the refinements of civilization." Contemporary conditions are defined by "this great irregularity" in the distribution of wealth, which is good, Carnegie says, but also "beyond our power to alter," and thus beyond critique, since "it is a waste of time to criticize the inevitable." On Carnegie's view, then, exceptionalism is acceptable, inevitable, and good. The rule is poverty, and there *should* be exceptions to it. That a few people are exceptionally wealthy despite the wide distribution of poverty is a consummation devoutly to be wished.

Vandana Shiva's eco-ethics protests such exceptionalism, and advocates an implicationalist position that would reorganize humans from the current growth economy into a sustenance economy. Shiva repudiates the ideal of *privatization*. In example after example (the building of dams, the patenting of seeds, "free trade" agreements) she shows the same pattern at work: the transfer of what had been part of "the commons" (that which is available and accessible to all) into the possession and control of a person or a corporation, one consequence of which is that others are excluded from it altogether, or excluded in the sense that they must now pay the possessor/ controller for access to it. She takes this process as flawed for at least two reasons. First, it violates the nature of the thing privatized, as in the case of water, which all humans need in order to live. The universality of the human need for water entails, Shiva contends, that water rightfully belongs to all, not to a few. Second, privatization strengthens the hegemony of market valuation over other forms of valuation. Water is transformed by privatization from something priceless (a necessary condition for human life) into something bought and sold, valued by a price.

Similarly, Shiva argues against the ideal of *growth*. Though the term obviously is intended to suggest that all are participating in a process of increase, Shiva depicts the process as actually one of redistribution rather than of increase, as consisting of the few appropriating for themselves what had been held in common. "Corporate globalization is based on new enclosures of the commons; enclosures which imply exclusions and are based on violence." Quite the opposite of what the word "growth" would imply, "globalization's transformation of all beings and resources into commodities robs diverse species and people of their rightful share of ecological, cultural, economic, and political space," giving the name "ownership" to what actually is dispossession. Because enclosure of the commons "displaces and disenfranchises people," it "creates scarcity for the many," effectively consolidating into the hands of a few what properly belongs to the many. "Growth" enforces and exaggerates the gap between wealth and poverty, thus extending exceptionalism.

Privatization and growth, Shiva contends, invert reality: under their sway, takings of the commons by individuals and by corporations are counted as ownership, and protections of the commons by the government are counted as takings. The result is poverty for "the commoners and the community": when they no longer have land, biodiversity, and water as "the source of livelihoods and economic security," the only resource left them is their labor. Enclosure polarizes, dividing "the common interest of people into the interest of the rich and powerful," for whom enclosure of the commons creates "progress, development, and growth," and the interest of the poor and marginalized, for whom "enclosures create new poverty, powerlessness, and, in the extreme, disposability." Enclosure, the engine of the global economy's structural violence and environmental destructiveness, is the material correlative (the outcome and the guarantee) of exceptionalism. It can be resisted (exception to it can be taken) only by an implicationalist approach that fosters a commons, open to all, not sequestered by the exceptional.

Another point would contrast humanism with posthumanism. Sartre's famous formulation, "existentialism is a humanism," could be amended to read "*exceptionalism* is a humanism." Sartre defends existentialism on the grounds that it enacts human exceptionalism. He identifies as the first principle of existentialism that "Man is nothing else but that which he makes of himself," and asserts it as implied by the principle "that man is of a greater dignity than a stone or a table." Humanity is exceptional, then, on Sartre's view, distinct from all else, the one existent in the universe "which propels itself towards a future and is aware that it is doing so," the one "project which possesses a subjective life, instead of being a kind of moss, or a fungus or a cauliflower." Humanity is autopoetic, and even cosmopoetic: "Before that projection of the self nothing exists." Sartre can defend existentialism as a humanism by demonstrating that existentialism affirms exceptionalism, because humanism itself affirms exceptionalism, and exceptionalism is the most favored element of humanism, one source of its broad appeal, its appearance of being self-evidently good. So broad is humanism's appeal, so evident is its seeming goodness, that to resist it something radical is needed. That something radical goes by the name "posthumanism."

Although he is careful to begin by pointing out the absence of consensus about just what "posthumanism" is or entails, Cary Wolfe identifies as "the fundamental anthropological dogma associated with humanism" the claim "that 'the human' is achieved by escaping or repressing not just its animal origins in nature, the biological, and the evolutionary, but more generally by transcending the bonds of materiality and embodiment altogether." In that sense, humanism is a totalizing exceptionalism: we humans are exceptions not only to the kingdom *animalia*, but even to nature and to the material world. Wolfe depicts posthumanism as opposing "the fantasies of disembodiment and autonomy," affirming instead "the embodiment and embeddedness of the human being in not just its biological but also its technical world" and naming "a historical moment in which the decentering of the human by its imbrication in technical, medical, informatic, and economic networks is increasingly impossible to ignore." Since exceptionalism, in the form of humanism, has been so hegemonic a premise, the result of entertaining a posthumanist conception, on Wolfe's view, is "a new reality: that the human occupies a new place in the universe," a universe populated by "nonhuman subjects." Posthumanism "means not the triumphal surpassing or unmasking of something but an increase in the vigilance, responsibility, and humility that accompany living in a world so newly, and differently, inhabited." Posthumanism, as Wolfe portrays it, is not a further exception to exceptionalism, not a more exceptional exceptionalism, but a taking exception to exceptionalism. It is implicationalist: we humans do not and cannot stand outside of or above our context, but are (and always have been) folded into it.

Rosi Braidotti's exposition emphasizes different aspects of posthumanism than Wolfe's does, but concurs with Wolfe in taking exception to exceptionalism. The posthuman, Braidotti says, deconstructs species supremacy, "but it also inflicts a blow to any lingering notion of human nature, *anthropos* and *bios*, as categorically distinct from the life of animals and non-humans, or *zoe*." Posthumanism finds us implicated, not exceptional. Humanism is premised on exceptionalism, as, Braidotti points out, Leonardo da Vinci's Vitruvian Man vividly illustrates. Vitruvian Man renews the Protagorean assertion that "man is the measure of all things," proposes "an ideal of bodily perfection which, in keeping with the classical dictum *mens sana in corpore sano*, doubles up as a set of mental, discursive and spiritual values," and emblematizes humanism "as a doctrine that combines the biological, discursive and moral expansion of human capabilities into an idea of teleologically ordained, rational progress." Humanism derives from, and in turn sustains, "faith in the unique, self-regulating and intrinsically moral powers of human reason." Braidotti's critical posthumanism, in contrast, undercuts humanistic exceptionalism, defining "the critical posthuman subject within an eco-philosophy of multiple belongings," proposing "an enlarged sense of inter-connection between self and others, including the non-human or 'earth' others, by removing the obstacle of self-centred individualism," and transposing "hybridity, nomadism, diasporas and creolization processes into means of re-grounding claims to subjectivity, connections and community among subjects of the human and the non-human kind." Like Wolfe's posthumanism, Braidotti's affirms implicationalism.

A third contrast might employ the terms "genius" and "genesis." Exceptionalism appears also as the prevalence and privilege of such ideals as "originality," "creativity," "inspiration," and "genius." Consider for instance Kant's paean to genius in the *Critique of Judgment*. He identifies genius with two definitions he presents as equivalent: genius is "the talent (or natural gift) which gives the rule to art"; it is "the innate mental disposition (*ingenium*) *through which* nature gives the rule to art." For Kant, then, the genius (the *person* who possesses and enacts the *quality* of genius) is exceptional. The genius is an agent of nature, a medium through which nature imposes its rules on human art. The rules that apply to everyone else do not apply to the genius: we all learn and follow rules for what we do, but the genius produces "that for which no definite rule can be given." Everyone else imitates examples, but the genius *is* an example, serving "as a standard or rule of judgment for others." The fruits of genius are inexplicable by any rules supposed to precede them. The "author of a product for which he is indebted to his genius," Kant declares, "does not know himself how he has come by his ideas; and he has not the power... to communicate it to others in precepts that will enable them to produce similar products." Genius is incommunicable; it is *exceptional.* If you can explain what you have done or thought, it was the result only of method or technique or learning or craft, not genius. Genius is not methodical, but an opposite of the methodical. Greatness in science is a difference only of degree, according to Kant, but the genius differs in kind from other humans: science is *acquired*, through learning, and thus in principle is available to anyone, but art is *given* by nature, available only to the recipient nature chooses. Scientific knowledge is the rule, artistic genius the exception.

Similarly, Coleridge treats the genius as an exception. Most people suffer "debility and dimness of the imaginative power, and a consequent necessity of reliance on the immediate impressions of the senses," which makes them "liable to superstition and fanaticism." Not warm enough by themselves, they gather into crowds "for a warmth in common, which they do not possess singly." The gathering provides the heat they need: "like damp hay, they heat and inflame by co-acervation; or like bees they become restless and irritable through the increased temperature of collected multitudes." In contrast to the many who congregate, the genius is egregious, in possession of the exceptional "and self-sufficing power of absolute *Genius*," a power that "is differenced from the highest perfection of talent, not by degree but by kind."

The eco-ethical and eco-aesthetic perspective articulated in poetic form in W. S. Merwin's *The Rain in the Trees* contrasts with the Kantian/ Coleridgean account of genius. Instead of locating creativity and the origin of language in the human quality most distinct from bees, Merwin imputes them to insects themselves. There is no genius, only genesis. We are not exceptional, not above even the life forms we typically think of as "low." Merwin connects past to future in an apostrophe "To the Insects": "we have been here so short a time," he begins, and "have forgotten what it is like to be you," but in the end "we turn into you." The insects were here long before us, and will be here long after. That historical and biological fact, as Merwin's poems understand it, entails the falsity of the exceptionalist concept of genius, and posits in its place an implicationalist vision of genesis: it is "the language of insects," rather than that of humans, that can "depict dark water and the veins of trees," that can convey "what is known at a distance," and so on. The insects have no need of genius, and no place for it. In place of genius, they enact genesis; in place of exceptionalism, implicationalism. It is *their* poetry, not ours, that wrote the world we live in, and their poetry, not ours, that will be "making music" long after we and our poetry sing no more.

The concept of genius draws on the antiquated (and exceptionalist) concept of "creation," but we have newer ways of understanding the dynamics of origin and derivation and change, such as evolution, endosymbiosis, autopoiesis, mutation, and emergence. Creation depicts each created kind as the volitional act of a god, and humans as the culminating kind. Everything exceptional, humans most of all. By contrast, the "origins of species" proposed by science all corroborate implicationalism rather than exceptionalism. Such aesthetic concepts as "creativity" and "genius" take creation as their metaphor; eco-aesthetics, as in the Merwin poem just cited, eschews creation, electing an implicationalist, rather than that exceptionalist, metaphor.

A final point would contrast positioning of humanity above nature versus within nature. Exceptionalism portrays humanity as the ruler of nature, with "dominion over the fish of the sea and the birds of the air." That portrayal itself takes various forms. One especially vivid form is the portrayal of humans as "managing" nature. The U.S. has a national governmental agency with this premise in its very title: the Bureau of Land Management. Its mission is "To sustain the health, diversity, and productivity of America's public lands for the use and enjoyment of present and future generations." It "administers" public land, and "manages" what it calls "sub-surface mineral estate." The Federal Land Policy and Management Act of 1976 mandates that the BLM "manage" public land and protect "resources." That mission and mandate is framed in the language of mastery and control, not the language of symbiosis (living with) but the language of supervision (watching over).

Historically, an even more vivid instance of this kind of exceptionalism was the concept of "manifest destiny," which offered a rationale for U.S. conquest of land and people from its Atlantic origins to the Pacific.

The vision of "manifest destiny" was prevalent in nineteenth-century U.S. discourse. In Amy S. Greenberg's words, "Starting in the late 1830s, American politicians asserted, and many citizens believed, that God had divinely ordained the United States to grow and spread across the continent. The course of American empire, supporters insisted, was both obvious (manifest) and inexorable (destined)." By the 1860s, the belief was established securely enough that it was embodied in institutions and policies, as for example in four major pieces of legislation from the year 1862, the Homestead Act, the Morrill Act (creating in each state a "land-grant" college to teach agriculture and military tactics), the Pacific Railroad Act, and the act establishing the U.S. Department of Agriculture. Each of those acts stood in reciprocal relation to manifest destiny: each took its justification from the concept of manifest destiny, as for instance the Homestead Act's institutionalization of the principle that if you can claim it you own it, and each served as confirmation of the *fact* of manifest destiny.

This reciprocal validation was a vicious circle, with very high human and ecological costs, but even at the time, there were implicationalist competitors to the profoundly exceptionalist ideal of manifest destiny, most obviously the eco-ethical vision of Thoreau, whose *Walden* was published in 1854, during the heyday of manifest destiny. Thoreau's eco-ethical vision emphasized his desire for acquaintance in place of acquisition. This is the contrast he establishes at the opening of the book, at the moment when he first "went down to Walden Pond" in March of 1845 to begin building his house there. Even this apparent act of exception — removing oneself to a form of solitude — is more crucially an act of implication, as Thoreau points out by noting that it is "difficult to begin without borrowing," which is "the most generous course" because it is the most reciprocal, one that "permit[s] your fellow-men to have an interest in your enterprise." The implication is ecological as well as social, accompanied as it is by "the lark and peewee and other birds," and resulting in sympathy between humanity and the natural world: "the winter of man's discontent was thawing as well as the earth" was thawing in those "pleasant spring days." His first task is cutting down some trees for lumber, and that act is implicationalist, Thoreau thinks, because it results not in acquisition but in acquaintance: "Before I had done I was more the friend than the foe of the pine tree, though I had cut down some of them, having become better acquainted with it."

Acquisition, the goal of manifest destiny, is a form of exceptionalism, a placing of oneself above the conditions that constrain other persons and things. Acquaintance, Thoreau's stated goal, is a form of implicationalism, a placing of oneself on a parity with other persons and things.

We (we Europeans, we Americans, we humans) are not exceptions, not exceptional. We are implicated in (folded into) one another's lives, and the workings of the biosphere. Eco-ethics and eco-aesthetics alike take up the challenge of coming to terms with that implication, by taking exception to exceptionalism.

Article 8:
Tell me someone I don't already know.

8.1: Poetry For Discovery

I write as I do in deference to a simple but inexhaustible truth: *Process may offer discovery.* A person throwing the I Ching seeks the vatic in patterns that arise from apparently random manipulation of counters (yarrow stalks, pennies...), and though I don't posit the work of a personified agent (the hand of chance, the hand of God) to fill with meaning the processes in which I participate as I write, I do expect to be rewarded with discovery when I trust the language, which though it be no person does have agency enough to tender revelation to anyone willing to attend. Process is one mode of attention, a way of plowing the ground of language, unearthing coins (coigns) and ordnance (ordonnance) and bones (boons) buried in it generations back, a way of fulfilling the imperative implicit in Robert Pogue Harrison's observation that "only by constantly retrieving the priority from which they arise" do "our words retain their capacity to bind, gather, collect, and mean."

Awash as we are in scandal and suasion (which celebrity has cellulite, which beer brings more babes, what inanity has been lately tweeted and by which dumbshit), small wonder we assume a lyric poem ought to gossip, sell you *my* feelings as yours, fondle anecdote, dotingly display another knick-knack in the curio cabinet. I don't doubt that poems may start with feeling and apply language to it, but the poems I want to write start with language and seek feeling there, are less Wordsworthian than Wittgensteinian: not emotion recollected in tranquility, but a bumping against the limits of language.

So, for example, "There is no avoiding" began not in my feelings but in someone else's words.

> awash with blushing textures, your hips, lipped lilies,
> sex as song. I feel lost here
> with just sequence to correct
> my view. Against so much glass
> starlight shuts a harsh door. On

> this my tentative guitar
> to tell by touch the passage
> to the river is to feel,
> obliquely on your body,
> the airs I sing. **There is no**
> **avoiding** oblivion,
> even for embodied gods,
> horses grazing side by side.
> The hand that anticipated everything —

This poem participates in a sequence entitled "All the One-Eyed Boys in Town," first published in *Legible Heavens*, then included, in a revised version, in *First Fire, Then Birds*. Some features of the sequence may be seen in this poem, such as circularity: each poem begins where the last left off, usually in the middle of a sentence, and ends, usually in the middle of another sentence, where the next begins, a pattern that includes the last poem's ending in the middle of a sentence that the first poem finishes, so that in principle any of the poems might serve for a starting point. The title (identified in bold) lives within the poem, rather than standing outside and above it. Together the titles themselves make a poem that appeared in the table of contents in *Legible Heavens* (though it makes itself more secretive in *First Fire, Then Birds*). Formally, the individual poems followed a simple syllabic pattern: 12-syllable first line, fourteen 7-syllable lines, 12-syllable last line. (In *First Fire, Then Birds*, they were condensed from fourteen to twelve 7-syllable lines.)

More often than not, I write poems in/as sequences. I marvel at the fractality of language, its manumission of meaning at any level — phoneme (*mmmmm!*), word (damn!), phrase (of course), clause, sentence, line, paragraph, work, oeuvre — so I work hard *not* to assume that a poem is the fundamental unit, whole and isolated. I try not to take for granted, in other words, that a poetry book ought to be a "collection" of poems. Within a poem, we expect any given word to have its connotations curved by other words in the poem (the nun-ness of "wimpling" in "The Windhover" contrasts with "dauphin" and "chevalier," its black-and-whiteness with "gold-vermilion"), but that also happens across poems (that the falcon wimples his wing "in his riding / Of the rolling level underneath him steady air" fathers-forth the "coiféd sisterhood" from which in "The Wreck of the Deutschland" came "the tall nun" whose call "To the men in the tops and the tackle rode over the storm's brawling"). I assume that any one of my poems ought to be modified by others of them, that my poetry ought to pursue arcs of meaning at all scales: within a line, and across books. Yes, I am building lines with words, and a poem with lines, but I am also building a sequence with poems.

The process of this sequence began with collection. I assembled a set of recent poetic sequences written by others. The list on the book's acknowledgments page begins: John Ashbery, *Shadow Train*; Anne Carson, *The Beauty of the Husband*; Debra Di Blasi, *Drought*; Rachel Blau DuPlessis, *Drafts 1-38: Toll*; Carol Frost, *Abstractions*; Forrest Gander, *Torn Awake*; and so on. From each listed work I collected phrases that engaged me, so in "There is no avoiding," which originates in phrases from C. D. Wright's *Deepstep Come Shining*, my notes look like this:

3: the ruby progression of taillights
4: it is unlike night
7: they would have been blue the eyes
8: ~~beautiful things~~ fill every vacancy
9: cold eyes are bad ~~to~~ eat
10: ~~there is no avoiding oblivion~~
13: ~~to correct the view~~
15: wonder who lives there
16: Get your bearings. Hear the trees.
21: crudely executed
22: ~~except for sex and song~~
23: take a mirror ~~to the river~~
25: never never never
27: this land became known as
28: I've been shouldering one rock at a time
29: of tenderness in the world
31: that they have a treeless afterlife
32: the fingers limber and lengthen
33: the sweating silver vase with sunflowers
35: if not the exact words
37: ~~there is so much glass~~ there

And so on, through p. 103. Next, I pieced portions of the collected text into a draft. Strikethroughs in the notes indicate passages used in the draft. By rule every word of the draft had to occur in the source text, so even a ligature like "to" in the draft came from a passage, here the passage from page 9. In revision, I applied various rules, such as insisting that the word "sequence" had to be inserted in place of some two-syllable word in each poem. I went through multiple rounds of word-shifting: removing a word from one poem, inserting it in place of a word with the same syllable count in the next poem, inserting the newly displaced word into the following poem, and so on. By the time the sequence was finished, a few phrases remained intact, but most had been modified. If the work succeeds, even unaltered phrases are "made new" by dislocation and relocation.

The process(es) behind this poem may appear to diminish the role of my subjectivity. To some, the processes will look dependent ("Those aren't even *your* words!") and mechanical ("You're not *writing*, you're just playing games"). Such objections, though, seem to me to beg the question, to take for granted the anecdotality of the lyric. Against the objection of dependency, I note only that *all* language is received and manipulated, and I appeal again, as often before, to Harold Bloom's apothegm, "The meaning of a poem can only be another poem." Against the objection that my processes are mechanical, I assert that even such apparently arbitrary rules as word shifting *in*clude my subjectivity rather than *ex*cluding it. I must choose the word in each case. (And I select or make up each rule.) The application of rules, I contend, creates multiple occasions for the assertion of my subjectivity, and for the reader's as well: in Jena Osman's formulation, "procedural poems have the capacity to produce aesthetic platforms from which the reader can take part in an act of receptive invention."

I don't presume to recollect emotion in tranquility, as if my emotion had been collected once, and now came trailing clouds of glory. I don't presume to express my feelings, as if I knew before the poem what my feelings are. I am not sending a gift by means of language, as one sends a box by FedEx. I assume instead that the *language* knows more than I do, that if I will treat it, Kantianly, also as an end and not merely as a means, it will reveal matters of consequence I might not otherwise know or feel or experience. I want in this way also to respect my poem's readers. My using the medium we share, the language, to report my experience or my internal state seems to me at high risk for condescension and narcissism. What reason has anyone else to care about or be edified by my feelings and thoughts? If, on the other hand, I find in the medium we share a means of discovery, *my* gaining from the shared medium some new perspective on my own experience seems to warrant hope that some similar new perspective might be available to others through the poem.

Or so I tell myself, to rationalize having done what there is no avoiding my doing.

8.2: Poetry For Self-Knowledge

This poem, from *Incident Light*, exemplifies a defining ambition of my work, in that it does not speak *of* me or *as* me, but does speak *to* me and *for* me:

> **You must have loved your dad.**
>
> He'd worn it out, the ragged cotton dress shirt
> he gave me to paint in in kindergarten,
> English all day in school but German at home.
> I wanted to sleep in that shirt, to wear it
> always, I cried when they made me take it off.
> I tried to talk, but knew only how to paint
> and cry. To this day a man in a white shirt
> makes me speak in primary colors and tears.

My fascination with the drama of self-understanding makes me less concerned with poetry's capacity to record how I felt than with its capacity to ask "who am I?" That capacity accounts for one sense in which poetry can be philosophical: not by presenting arguments in pretty language — Kant with a lilt — but by attending to the Delphic/Socratic imperative to "know thyself."

That charge, to "know thyself," has binding force because how one answers "who am I?" stands in reciprocal relationship with how one answers "what ought I do?" The most elemental human dramas occur in (and *as*) the truing of one's circumstances, one's actions, and one's answers to those two questions: the resolution of dissonance between one's answers to the two questions (I think of myself as an ecologically-minded citizen, so I ought not be an employee of a state whose economy rides on mineral extraction), between one's circumstances and one's answer to "who am I?" (we in the U.S. believe we are a mighty nation, but 9/11 said we are a vulnerable nation), or between one's actions and one's answer to "what ought I do?" (I ignore the panhandler's request for money, but I ought to be generous).

The commonality that makes possible my identification with another person, and consequently my learning from someone else's experience, not only from my own, is not circumstances per se, but the attempt to true circumstances with self-understanding. *King Lear* and *Oedipus Rex* have the force they do, not because my circumstances resemble Cordelia's or Oedipus' circumstances (never have I been a princess, never King of Thebes) but because Cordelia, Oedipus, and I each must reconcile our self-understanding with our circumstances. Failure to achieve such reconciliation (as Lear and Oedipus both so flagrantly fail) invites, or maybe just *is*, tragedy.

I say all that to say this: I read as hyperbole Rilke's assertion early in his *Letters to a Young Poet* that "A work of art is good if it has sprung from necessity. In this nature of its origin lies the judgment of it: there is no other." Still, I did have the sense about *Incident Light* that it was necessary, that it *had* to be written. Not because my circumstances resemble the circumstances of the book's protagonist (they don't much) but because her drama — the challenge her circumstances presented to her self-understanding — is, like that of Cordelia or Oedipus, elemental.

Incident Light listens for the life of Petra Soesemann, an extraordinary artist with whom I have enjoyed a long friendship nourished by periods during which we have been professional colleagues, first at the Kansas City Art Institute, then, years later, at the Cleveland Institute of Art. You might guess what drew my attention to Petra's life *as* a story that had to be told, if you knew that Petra's dad, who passed away quite a few years ago, and her mother, who is still alive, both are blue-eyed German blonds, but that Petra herself has dark features: olive skin, dark hair, dark eyes. Petra was forty-nine years old when she learned what in retrospect seems obvious, that the dad who had raised her from birth, the dad she had adored, was not her biological father. It turns out, of course, that her mother had had a brief affair with a Turkish man, who is Petra's biological father.

I call Petra's story "elemental" because her circumstances (that new information about her birth) so abruptly challenged previously secure-seeming aspects of her answer to the question "who am I?" It imposed a new self-understanding. For almost fifty years, she thought that her paternal nature and nurture had come from the same source, but then one day she learned they had not. In this way her story resembles *Lear* and *Oedipus*: it poses the question, what happens if I learn something tomorrow that makes me understand my origins in a totally new way? I myself probably will not ever be told that my biological father was not the father who raised me, any more than I will be anointed King of Thebes, but I might be confronted one day with other circumstances, the nature of which I cannot anticipate, that will make me rethink my ways of answering "who am I?" So Petra's singular life also has a universality: it speaks to and for other people's lives, including my own.

Petra's story is elemental, but also very intimate and personal, not something to which I have any rights, so for a long time I took no action except to keep thinking about it. Finally, though, I asked Petra for permission to write about — to try to write *into* — her experience. Of the forms of research toward the book, interviews of Petra proved the most important and most generative. Like many other poems in *Incident Light*, "You must have loved your dad." derived from something Petra told me during those interviews. At one point, I asked her "What's your favorite item of clothing that you no longer possess? That you once had but don't have any more?" She began to talk about various shirts: a shirt she'd worn in college, that she had bought in the boy's department at the store; a lucky pink driving shirt. That led her to mention an old white dress shirt her father had given her to paint in when she was a small child. For a long time, she told me,

> I had a real thing for men's white shirts, and I think it had something to do with when I went to nursery school, and it was part of learning English, that whole thing. My Dad gave me an old white dress shirt, and it was what I wore when we did painting. And of course I loved painting. And the painting and the dress shirt and this struggle between English and German and trying to make myself understood, it all got mooshed together somehow. And with the Dad thing, too. I wouldn't take the shirt off for anything.

I would cry when I had to take the shirt off. I wanted to sleep in it. And somehow that stuck with me. I'm sure that it linked up with the Dad thing in a more subconscious way than I realized, because I had a real thing for white shirts for a long time. I mean, men who would wear white shirts, and the right kind of shirts. And it would be, you know, I wouldn't think about it, and then I would realize it, and every time I would realize it, it would be like the first time. It was absurd. I still really like white shirts.

Just as Petra's "big" story is compelling, so are the many "small" stories she told during the interviews. This one had many features I wanted to capture: Petra's gravitating to art at an early age; the experience of moving back and forth between languages; how strongly her Dad continues as an influence in her life, even though he passed away some years ago; the ways early experiences linger, informing later experiences; and so on. But *how* to let all those aspects of the anecdote retain their life in a poem? How (in the terms that introduce this essay) compose a poem that speaks *of* and *as* Petra, but *to* and *for* me?

For the book as a whole, the *how* question got solved only after long delay. I tried various approaches to the project, but my prose consistently came out "flat," archival, dutifully arranging the facts themselves but not conveying their emotional weight, and my poetry came out "stiff," artificial, self-indulgently drawing attention to itself and away from its subject. The false starts accumulated, and the months of waiting for traction turned into years. Then, just before I was to begin a short residency, I happened to read Francisco Goldman's "The Great Bolaño," an essay-review of four books by Roberto Bolaño. In the process of discussing Bolaño's *The Savage Detectives*, Goldman notes that "Juan Garcìa Madero, the seventeen-year-old narrator of the diary that makes up the novel's 124-page first section, titled 'Mexicans Lost in Mexico,' is an orphan who lives with his middle-class aunt and uncle, a law student enrolled in a poetry workshop at the university. He knows what a *rispetto* is (an Italian form of verse composed of eight lines with eleven syllables each), but the workshop teacher does not." *I* hadn't known, either, what a rispetto is, until that moment.

There are other elements to the rispetto: for instance, like the sonnet it has various rhyme schemes. But I decided to adopt only those two constraints, eight lines and eleven syllables per line, and suddenly, after years of trying but failing to write the book, in the two-week residency the whole book poured out. Those two constraints were enough to lend formal continuity to the project without suffocating it. The flexibility within the poems and the similarity across them permitted very compact individual poems to "speak to each other" without a lot of additional explanatory material, and also allowed for *dis*similarity, for the presence among the many rispettos of a few poems that take other shapes.

That global solution to the *how* question, the rispetto as the project's formal vehicle, still left each individual poem with its local version of *How?* For this poem in particular, the prompt came from Galway Kinnell's "Prayer," a three-line poem in which the central line uses the same word three times in a row: "...is is is..." The long shadow of Strunk and White urges a writer to *eliminate* the copula, to regard it as a weak, empty verb, but Kinnell goes to the opposite extreme: he stacks three on top of one another. From Kinnell's example I took permission to stack instances of "in." I only got two in a row, not three, but the poem wanted emphasis on the relation between internal and external, and saying "in in" allowed that to happen. It drew attention to the shirt's function as an "objective correlative," an external object that represents an internal emotional state.

The story of this poem's composition leads to no grandiose, wholly original moral. Still, I find in it something instructive, something I think it good to remind myself of. I listened to Petra from the start, but I heard what I heard from her only when I found a vehicle fit for the hearing of it. If the renewal demanded by Rilke's "You must revise your life" is perpetual, so is that imposed by this dictum of poetic craft: You must relearn to hear.

Article 9:
One word changes, one word changes everything.

9.1: Poetry Against Correspondence

In certain situations, we have reason to value instances of one-to-one correspondence: you have nine players on your co-ed softball team, and the game is scheduled to start in a few minutes, so thank goodness our catcher is on her way to join the other eight of us on my team who are here already. In some matters, one-to-one correspondence presents itself as given by nature rather than chosen by humans: conception results from the union of one egg with one sperm. There are such cases, and we often notice and appreciate them, but neither the existence of the cases nor our appreciating them entails that one-to-one correspondence does hold, or ought to hold, always.

Even where we *expect* one-to-one correspondence, an alternative may not be always or altogether bad. When I attend a performance of a play, for example, I expect a one-to-one correspondence between actors and roles, and probably I will assume, unreflectively, that one-to-one correspondence is the ideal. I will expect one person to play Hamlet, another to play Ophelia. The most memorable performance I have seen, though, of a Shakespeare play was a version of *The Tempest* performed by four actors, each playing multiple parts, signaling changes between roles by adjustments in how he/she wore his/her sweater (the actors were wearing khakis and sweaters, not period dress). Other examples, such as early Greek tragedy, further emphasize that a one-to-one correspondence between actors and roles in drama is not necessary, universal, or always self-evidently best.

There is reason to alter the widely-held judgment among English speakers that identical rhyme is a flawed, inept derivative of "perfect" rhyme. Identical rhyme is a valid, worthy form of rhyme, able to register, as other forms of rhyme cannot, the multiplicity of identity.

Rhyme is not exclusively ornamental, a decorative supplement adorning an otherwise plain language use, detached from the ideas and contexts and political entanglements of that language. Alternative performances and accounts of rhyme advance alternative philosophical understandings.

Sara Ahmed performs one such alternative when she describes the organization of her book *Willful Subjects* as "threads of argument that are woven together and tied up somewhat loosely." She notes that she has "used echoes and repetitions across the chapters," relying "on the *sound* of connection to build up a case from a series of impressions" in a way that makes the writing "poetic as well as academic." Her approach, she protests, is intentional and purposeful. Calling it *poetic* "is not to say there is no reason in the rhyme. In structuring this book," she says, "my aim has been to thicken gradually my account of the sociality of will." Rather than following the structural expectations for argumentation that she anticipates in her audience, according to which the logic would be visible as *sequence*, as steps in a destination-enforcing progression, Ahmed chooses rhyme as the bearer of her book's logic, not on the grounds that it will lead readers inexorably to a conclusion but on the grounds that it will thicken her account.

Similarly, Leslie Scalapino is speaking broadly of poetry, inclusive of all its techniques and devices, not exclusively of rhyme, when she says, "In language horizontal and vertical time can occur at the same moment." Her claim about poetic language in general applies to rhyme in particular. As in Ahmed, so in Scalapino, rhyme (like other instances and elements of the poetic) is not exclusively or primarily ornamental. For Scalapino, it is one locus for the convergence of synchrony and diachrony. It functions the way prayer functions in Augustine, as a means through which we who are finite and temporal can mimic the creative power of that which is infinite and eternal. Like Augustine's God, Scalapino's poetic language is eternal not in the sense of limitless duration but in the sense of unqualified simultaneity, the presence of all times at once: "Remembering everything, all layers at the same time, writing *is* the mind's operations *per se and* imitation of it at the same time." This dual capacity of poetic language, to impose simultaneity and to merge noesis with mimesis, enables poetry to do "the work of philosophy" by being "writing that is conjecture."

Ahmed and Scalapino recognize that rhyme is philosophical. It proposes an ontology. My point here is that the ontology proposed varies with the type of rhyme employed. Perfect rhyme pretends linear time, progression, propulsion from beginning to end. Identical rhyme pretends cyclical time, ongoingness, return. Perfect rhyme assumes that identity is singular. Identical rhyme assumes that identity is multiple. Perfect rhyme is associative: it brings one thing into proximity with another. Identical rhyme is distributive: it multiplies and explicates, seeing more than one aspect to what presents itself as if it were one thing.

In English, the prototypical understanding of "rhyme" is captured by the definition in the *New Princeton Encyclopedia of Poetry and Poetics*: "the linkage in poetry of two syllables at line end [...] which have identical medial vowels and final consonants but differ in initial consonant(s)—syllables which, in short, begin differently and end alike." The many variants (feminine rhyme, apocopated rhyme, and so on) all are taken as deviations from, and ineffective approximations to, this prototype, which has come to be called "perfect rhyme."

Citing with apparent approval the *Oxford English Dictionary*'s definition of rhyme, which describes that prototype, emphasizing that "the last stressed vowel and any sounds following it are the same, while the sound or sounds preceding it are different," Edward Hirsch asserts that "There is something charged and magnetic about a good rhyme, something both unsuspected and inevitable, something utterly surprising and unforeseen and yet also binding and necessary. It is as if the poet had called up the inner yearning of words to find each other." Hirsch's comment reveals that the prototypical description of rhyme represents not only a consensus about what makes a rhyme a rhyme but also a criterion for what makes a rhyme a *good* rhyme. The prototype of rhyme is descriptive *and* prescriptive.

The prescriptive aspect of the designation "perfect rhyme" appears in scholarly accounts, but also in popular ones. At this writing, the first item in a Google search for "identical rhyme" is the website of Dr. L. Kip Wheeler, a professor who notes for his students that "[m]any poets frown upon identical rhyme as unartful," but qualifies others' judgment by observing that identical rhyme can "add emphasis to a poetic passage." Wikipedia extends the pattern, noting that identical rhymes "are considered less than perfect in English poetry," but offering the qualification that they "are valued more highly in other literatures," giving the example of rime riche in French poetry. In the Wikipedia entry, identical rhyme is "inferior" to perfect rhyme, unless it extends "even farther back than the last stressed vowel. If it extends all the way to the beginning of the line, so that there are two lines that sound identical, then it is called a 'holorhyme' ('For I scream/For ice cream')," and in poetics "these would be considered *identity*, rather than rhyme."

A website called *English Language & Usage Stack Exchange*, which describes itself as "a question and answer site for linguists, etymologists, and serious English language enthusiasts," directly poses the question "Why are identical rhymes inferior in English poetry?," addressing it in the form of open dialogue. Answers proposed by participants in the dialogue include:

- The "mere repetition of a word... may indicate a lack of creativity."
- Identical rhymes are "boring, as are all repetitions but homozygous twins."
- Identical rhymes resemble puns, which are "the lowest form of humor."
- Identical rhymes fail to achieve novelty.
- "I suspect that the psychological effect of rhymed poetry is such that the pleasant effect is mediated by an expectation of a patterned phonological difference, which is not met by absolute phonological identity."
- Identical rhyme is conspicuous, and "conspicuous poetry sounds awkward."

However plausible or implausible any one of the answers may be, each grants the assumption made in the very form of the question, namely that identical rhymes *are* inferior.

Not all sources confine themselves exclusively to the popular imputation of inherent inferiority to identical rhyme. The *New Princeton Encyclopedia* carefully supplements its narrow prototypical definition with a broader, more open definition, describing rhyme as "the phonological correlation of differing semantic units at distinctive points in verse," and rationalizing the broader definition on the grounds that "it is essential that the definition not be framed solely in terms of sound, for that would exclude the cognitive function." Rhyme, it continues, "calls into prominence simultaneously a complex set of responses based on *identity* and *difference*." Sameness points to difference: "the likeness of the rhyming syllables (at their ends) points up their difference (at their beginnings). The phonic semblance (and difference) then points up semantic semblance or difference." In the *Encyclopedia*'s account, rhyme makes difference and identity "antinomian": "they mutually entail one another." Sound is sense. Rhyme "is not, therefore, a merely sonal phenomenon: it deploys sound similarity as the means to semantic and structural ends." The *New Princeton Encyclopedia*'s entry does not *make* the claim that identical rhyme has value, but does *open onto* the possibility.

Thomas Hobbes articulates a widely-held view, namely that establishing and maintaining a one-to-one ratio between words and their referents results in truth, and that failure to do so results in dangerous and harmful error. Because truth "consisteth in the right ordering of names in our affirmations," he says, a person who seeks truth "had need to remember what every name he uses stands for," or (here the danger) "he will find himselfe entangled in words, as a bird in lime-twiggs; the more he struggles, the more belimed." Where the one-to-one ratio holds, words are "Perspicuous" and "The Light of humane minds," because they have been "by exact definitions first snuffed, and purged from ambiguity." Truth is achieved, and reality disclosed, on Hobbes's view, by disambiguation. One word, one referent, one truth. Multiplicity muddles and deceives.

Besides the obvious problem that in fact words do not operate in a one-to-one correspondence with what they represent (as the number of definitions for each word in any standard dictionary suggests), there is the more abstract problem that in principle words *could not* so operate. There are far too many things out there for us to have a word for each. A one-to-one correspondence between words and representables would face the Borgesian problem of the map that, to *represent* the world accurately, would have to *be* the world. A perfect vocabulary would not be a vocabulary; it would be the world. Perfect representation would not be representation; it would be reality.

There are implications to insistence on one-to-one correspondence. It is no accident that Hobbes's insistence on one-to-one correspondence between words and their referents forms part of a larger argument for unmitigated totalitarianism in government, in the form of unqualified sovereignty of a single leader. Singular identity readily becomes monolithic identity. A caricatured version of such monolithic identity occurs in Samuel P. Huntington's characterization of "the West" as a single, unified cultural identity, constant across changes in time and context. The dividing line between West and non-West, Huntington contends, "has moved several hundred miles east" from the Iron Curtain to "the line separating the peoples of Western Christianity, on the one hand, from Muslim and Orthodox peoples on the other." The dividing line has moved, but the division has remained, unchanged. This cultural essence makes it inevitable, according to Huntington, that among postcommunist societies in the former Soviet Union, "Those with Western Christian heritages are making progress toward economic development and democratic politics; the prospects for economic and political development in the Orthodox countries are uncertain; the prospects in the Muslim republics are bleak." That the identity is singular allows it to be monolithic; that it is monolithic suits it (because any monism denies change) to Huntington's purpose of rationalizing the current distribution of global wealth.

One might work backward, though, to show that this standard assumption of singular identity, however widely held, cannot stand scrutiny. Attentive inquiry reveals identity as multiple. This is true in regard to political entities, so Amartya Sen replaces Huntington's monolithic, singular-identity account of cultural history with an account that recognizes the multiplicity of identity. "The difficulty," Sen notes, with Huntington's "thesis of the clash of civilizations begins well before we come to the issue of an inevitable clash; it begins with the presumption of the unique relevance of a singular classification." Civilizational clash could seem inevitable, that is, only if the civilizations are construed through a reductive and essentializing lens, according to which, despite "our *diverse diversities*, the world is suddenly seen not as a collection of people, but as a federation of religions and civilizations." Humans are not exhaustively described by a single identity, nor are humans confined to affiliation with a single group. One person might "be a British citizen, of Malaysian origin, with Chinese racial characteristics, a stockbroker, a nonvegetarian, an asthmatic, a linguist, a bodybuilder, a poet, an opponent of abortion, a bird-watcher, an astrologer, and one who believes that God created Darwin to test the gullible." Such a person, of course, would belong to many groups that might be relevant to issues of identity (British citizens, asthmatics, bodybuilders, and so on), not to mention countless others, sublime or absurd, of little relevance or consequence ("the set of people in the world who were born between nine and ten in the morning, local time"). The upshot is that singular identity is mistaken, both descriptively and prescriptively: "when our differences are narrowed into one devised system of uniquely powerful categorization," we all are diminished, the world is made "much more flammable," and our shared humanity is "savagely challenged."

As it does culturally and politically, so also ontologically does multiplicity of identity assert itself. Although many philosophers (such as Hobbes) have been among those most insistent on singularity of identity, a few have recognized multiplicity. Wittgenstein, for example, modifies Joseph Jastrow's duck-rabbit, in order to illustrate what he calls "noticing an aspect," which he describes in this way: "I contemplate a face, and then suddenly notice its likeness to another. I *see* that it has not changed; and yet I see it differently."

Wittgenstein notes that if I had "seen the duck-rabbit simply as a picture-rabbit from the first," I would not have answered the question "What do you see here?" by replying that "Now I am seeing it as a picture-rabbit." I would simply have replied, "A picture-rabbit," and, pressed further, "I should have explained by pointing to all sorts of pictures of rabbits, should perhaps have pointed to real rabbits, talked about their habits, or given an imitation of them." In other words, I would have taken the one *aspect* I see as the singular, exhaustive *identity* of the figure. If I saw the duck and the rabbit, I would report the ambiguity by locating it in myself, as an ambiguity of perception ("I see it as a duck and as a rabbit"), but if I saw only the rabbit, I would locate the identity in the figure ("It's a rabbit"). That discrepancy in how I would report my experience reveals the cultural prejudice that singular identity is objective and real, multiple identity imaginary and subjective. But the duck-rabbit itself reveals the falsity of the prejudice: duck and rabbit are equally present in the figure, whether or not I see and acknowledge both identities.

From Wittgenstein, one might take multiplicity of identity as a liminal pheonomenon, one curiosity among the many that philosophy has not well accounted for. Jan Zwicky, though, develops an approach she calls "lyric philosophy" with multiplicity of identity as one of its central premises. Wisdom, she says, "has to do with the grasp of wholes that occupy the same space yet are different. This life, as opposed to that." Zwicky takes the Nekker Cube as an exemplum.

In it, two wholes occupy the same space yet are different. In one whole, the square on the right is the closest face of the cube, and in the other the square on the left is closer. Recognition of this multiplicity is not ancillary or idle, on Zwicky's view: "To be wise is to be able to grasp another form of life without abandoning one's own; to be able to translate experience into and out of two original tongues," resisting translation as a form of reduction. Zwicky speaks of "gestalt shift," such experiences as "seeing how an assemblage of parts must go together, recognizing an old friend in an unfamiliar setting, and understanding a metaphor," as "the original of meaning."

One might question the value judgment about identical rhyme by asking why identical rhyme at the *end* of lines is typically construed as flawed and ineffective, but identical rhyme at the *beginning* of lines — i.e., anaphora — is typically construed as artful and effective. Examples of widely-esteemed instances of anaphora include the Biblical Psalms, the "Beautitudes" from the Gospel of Matthew, Christopher Smart's *Jubilate Agno*, and Martin Luther King's "I have a dream" speech. Why do we find such instances of "identical rhyme" at the *beginning* of lines incantatory and effective, but find identical rhyme at the *end* of lines flawed and unsatisfying?

The affinity between identical rhyme and anaphora reveals that our categories are not clearly demarcated and mutually exclusive, but instead blur into one another. The category "rhyme" displays what George Lakoff, following Eleanor Rosch, calls "prototype effects": asymmetries among members of a category, according to which language users treat certain members of the category as "more representative of the category than other members. For example," Lakoff reports, "robins are judged to be more representative of the category bird than are chickens, penguins, and ostriches, and desk chairs are judged to be more representative of the category chair than are rocking chairs, barber chairs, beanbag chairs, or electric chairs."

The more representative members are considered prototypical. Lakoff argues that "we organize our knowledge by means of structures called *idealized cognitive models*, or ICMs," which include background assumptions that may fit the world with relatively much or relatively little precision. Lakoff borrows from Charles Fillmore the example of the English word "bachelor." The idealized cognitive model attached to "bachelor" (an ICM characterized by the definition "unmarried adult man") fits the world, Lakoff suggests, with relatively little precision. It carries background assumptions about heterosexual monogamy, marriage, marriageable age, courtship rituals, and so on, that are far from universal. It is easy to identify cases in which the fit is poor: a male participant in a long-term homosexual couple relationship, for example, is an unmarried adult man, but not a bachelor. The ICM of rhyme also fits the world poorly. Its treatment of "perfect rhyme" as more representative than "identical rhyme" of the category "rhyme" is unwarranted. Robins are not *better* birds than penguins, and perfect rhyme is not better rhyme than identical rhyme.

William Meredith employs identical rhyme in "The Illiterate." The poem follows the conventions of the Petrarchan sonnet, but its end rhymes are almost all of them identical rhymes instead of perfect rhymes: man / hand / hand / man / anyone / means / means / someone // him / word / beloved / him / words / beloved. The poem introduces its conceit in the first line. "Touching your goodness," Meredith begins, "I am like a man / Who turns a letter over in his hand." It then dismisses one guess about why he does so (because the handwriting is unfamiliar), and gives the real reason: because the man "Has never had a letter from anyone," and consequently finds the letter mysterious and intimidating, as any illiterate person would find any writing (recall Bellerophon's awe and wonder at the writing he carries in *The Iliad*). The recipient of the letter imagines various possibilities for what it might mean (did his uncle leave him the farm? have his parents died? does the girl he loves love him in return?), and the poem concludes by asking "What would you call his feeling for the words / That keep him rich and orphaned and beloved?"

The identical rhyme in the poem correlates with multiplicity of meaning for the rhyming words. "Hand," for instance, refers first to the limb on a human body ("turns a letter over in his hand"), and then to script ("the hand / Was unfamiliar"). Or, again, "means" refers first to sense or significance ("afraid of what it means"), and then to instrumentality or agency ("no other means / To find out"). By turning words over as the illiterate man turns the letter over, the poem performs a Wittgensteinian seeing-and-then-seeing-differently, an Ahmedian "thickening." By using its rhyming words first in one way and then in another, it eschews the ideal of truth that Hobbes advocates, which results from disambiguation, and joins Zwicky's ideal of wisdom in resisting reduction, seeing more than one whole in the same "space."

One might trace the same embodiment of multiple identity in other instances of identical rhyme such as Elizabeth Bishop's "One Art," employing as it does the received form of the villanelle, whose line repetitions entail identical rhyme. The identical rhyme word "master," for example, might mean either to get good at or to overcome, and the speaker in the poem wants to do both: her protestation that she wants to master losing in the sense of getting good at it carries as its shadow her wish that she could master losing in the sense of overcoming it. To disambiguate the word "master," to use it in the poem only one time and with one meaning, to rhyme it only with perfect rhymes but not with identical rhymes, would defuse the poem's emotional charge; the identical rhyme, the recurrence of and emphasis on the word "master," the drawing-out of its multiple meanings, strengthens that emotional charge. An analogous case could be made about the identical rhyme in Robert Frost's "Stopping by Woods on a Snowy Evening": to repeat and emphasize the word "sleep" draws out the double entendre, sleep literally as sleep and sleep metaphorically as death, on which the emotional tenor of the poem depends. The first time the speaker says, "And miles to go before I sleep," the reader sees one whole occupying the space of sleep, and the second time, another whole. Again, Robert Creeley's poem "Four," which consists of the sentence "Before I die" repeated four times, exemplifies both the blurring of categories (Is it identical rhyme? Yes. Is it repetition? Yes.) and the multiplicity of identity, the presence of difference in the same (Does "Before I die" mean the same thing the first time it is said as it does the fourth time? Hardly.).

One might say of poems what William Gass says of "well-regulated fictions," namely that in them, "most things are *overdetermined*." Identical rhyme, by manifesting that overdetermination, fulfills at least that one broad poetic ideal. A poem manipulates identity and difference. In perfect rhyme, difference is present in the (different) words used; in identical rhyme, difference is present in the (different) uses of the (identical) word.

In a reflection on a stanza from Baudelaire, Laurent Dubreuil watches translators of the poem into English engage in a few of the "innumerable ways of not reading what this text is saying." Dubreuil begins with the English translation by William Aggeler: "I am the wound and the dagger! / I am the blow and the cheek! / I am the member and the wheel, / Both the victim and the executioner!" Dubreuil gives the original as: "Je suis la plaie et le couteau! / Je suis le soufflet et la joue! / Je suis les membres et la roue, / Et la victime et le borreau!" The translators, he observes, attempt by various means "to attenuate the cognitive 'scandal' of Baudelaire's piece." The poem pushes against the principle of non-contradiction, and Dubreuil's point is that the translators consistently lose their nerve, mollifying the poem's resistance and affirming the unqualified authority of principle of non-contradiction. The translators "rely on a conventional acceptance of cognitive logicality." They "attempt to reduce the intellective challenge of the poem and, in this, ratify the rationalistic program of cognitive enclosure." My point is analogous. Treating perfect rhyme as, well, perfect, and identical rhyme as one of its imperfect derivatives reduces the intellective challenge posed by identical rhyme, which questions the widely-held but typically unexamined premise that truth derives from establishing and maintaining a one-to-one correspondence between word and referent, and resists the inclination toward reducing identity to singularity.

Identity establishes two of the most basic limits to thought. Tautology ("It is what it is") and contradiction ("It is and it is not") both involve identity and difference. Identical rhyme operates with adjacency to both. In this regard, it is "primitive," recalling an aspect of presocratic thought that was suppressed in later philosophy by the preoccupation with establishing and maintaining a distinction between philosophy and sophistry. Heraclitus allows multiplicity to be present in identity, but when Charles H. Kahn translates the fragment he numbers L, he cannot bring himself to keep the identical rhyme (the repetition) in Heraclitus' original, so he makes *hetera kai hetera* not into "other and other" but into "other and still other": "As they step into the same rivers, other and still other waters flow upon them." Similarly, Parmenides brushes against tautology and contradiction with his declaration that *estin ê ouk estin*, but Kirk and Raven disambiguate the particle ê, which means ambiguously "and" and/or "or," with their translation "it *is* or it is not." Instead of capturing the double meaning in Parmenides' original (as one might by simply leaving out the particle, translating "is, is not"), Kirk and Raven kill the duck to feed the rabbit. They transform Parmenides' brush with contradiction into an affirmation of the principle of non-contradiction, taking it, in that sense, as far as possible from the original.

Perfect rhyme presents difference in difference. Identical rhyme presents difference in the same. Both hold value. Devaluation of identical rhyme is unwarranted prejudice.

9.2: Poetry Against Fungibility

You'd think by now we'd have named them all, the means available to writers, selection from and application of which we call craft, but here I nominate for our list one that until now has gone unidentified. I call it "the voltic word." About this means I have more questions than certitudes, so I introduce it not by a fixed definition followed by a set of expository declarations but by proposing two prototypes and posing a few questions.

The prototypes come from Robert Hayden's "Those Winter Sundays" and Gwendolyn Brooks's "Sadie and Maud." Both poems are familiar: widely anthologized, often studied in poetry classes, loved by many readers, myself among them. I pair them here to highlight a previously unremarked perfection of craft that they share. The perfection is this: each contains a word that in another context might be innocuous, even a throwaway word, but that in its particular usage in the poem implies much more than it says, *so* much that it transforms the whole poem. In Hayden, the word occurs in the first line of the poem; in Brooks, in the last. In both, though, the implications of the word extend across the whole poem, greatly intensifying its emotional force.

I mean "prototypes" in the special sense that word bears in linguistics, as elucidated by George Lakoff. Drawing on others' prior research, Lakoff argues that we organize our knowledge into categories not primarily by testing items against definitions to create clearly-bounded sets of things, but by arraying instances around prototypes. I might not be able to offer a definition of "bird" that would satisfy an ornithologist, but I don't *need* a definition. I use the concept quite successfully without a definition, because I have learned to employ robins and sparrows as my prototypes for a category that also includes such oddballs as penguins and puffins and pelicans. Prototypes can serve not only as *typical* examples, the way robins and sparrows serve as typical birds, but also as *ideal* examples. Jackie Robinson, for instance, is a prototype of "athlete" not because he is *typical* of what athletes in fact most often are like, but because he exemplifies an ideal of what athletes might be. The Hayden and Brooks examples may be prototypes in the sense that they are typical, but that is not the most important sense here. I present them as prototypes of the voltic word because they are *ideal* examples of the category. I want ideal examples, rather than typical ones, because my ultimate aim is not skill at spotting voltic words in others' work but skill at using them in my own.

In Hayden, the voltic word is "too." "Those Winter Sundays" begins, not with the line "On Sundays my father got up early," but with the line "Sundays too my father got up early." The "too" already indicates, in the poem's second word, much of what the rest of the poem will unpack. My father does not lie in bed late most days of the week, rising finally at noon when his butler brings his smoking jacket and his breakfast of two poached eggs in china cups, excepting only Sunday, the butler's day off, when Dad bounds eagerly out of bed to enjoy the adventure of roughing it by lighting the fire himself. Nor does father head to the depot five days a week in his tailored suit and silk tie to catch the downtown train so he can fulfill his banker's hours, leaning back in a leather chair in his sunny twelfth-floor office, feet crossed on his desk, sipping coffee brought him by his secretary. Those scenarios would remain live through the line "On Sundays my father got up early," but in the poem's actual first line the "too" precludes all such possibilities. It says my father works *six* days a week, not five: he *never* gets to sleep in. The presence of "too" makes the blueblack cold not an exception to the conditions that govern the rest of his experience but the rule, one his Sunday mornings inside the family home share with his hard manual labor that he endures every other day of the week. That it is Sundays *too* intensifies the emotion of the poem by emphasizing that the speaker's father did not perform only the parts of fatherhood he found pleasant, and only *because* he found fatherhood pleasant. He performed his fatherly role on the terms that Kant says are the only virtuous ones: he performed his duties *because they were duties*, whether he enjoyed them or not. All this (life circumstances, social setting, ethical framework) follows from the voltic word "too."

In Brooks, the voltic word is "this." Throughout the poem, the speaker stays in third person, describing both Sadie and Maud from outside. "Maud went to college. / Sadie stayed at home," the poem tells us, continuing with descriptions such as Sadie's being "one of the livingest chits / In all the land" (her standing among the livingest guaranteed by the fact that she bore two illegitimate daughters) and Maud's being "a thin brown mouse." But "Sadie and Maud" does not end by saying of Maud that "She is living all alone / In her old house," or "all alone / In an old house," as the rest of the poem would lead the reader to expect. The ending of "Sadie and Maud" still refers to Maud in the third person (*she* is living all alone), but the last line's use of "this" instead of "her" or "an" reveals that the speaker all along has been Maud: "She is living all alone / In this old house." Because it is not disclosed until the end of the poem that the speaker is Maud herself, we readers have to reconsider everything that has gone before, registering the poem's critique of Sadie not as that of a disinterested "judicious spectator" but as that of a sister who has been affected by Sadie's decisions, and registering the poem's judgments about Maud not as critique from outside but as self-critique. The whole poem changes once we reach "this." Like "too" in "Those Winter Sundays," so "this" in "Sadie and Maud" intensifies the emotion of the poem. From the neutral observational viewpoint readers have been permitted through the poem, suddenly we are thrust into the viewpoint of Maud, who recognizes only after it is too late that her sister has been seizing the day and that she herself has missed her chance. We see that Sadie has lived her life fully, and that Maud has let her life pass her by, but because of the voltic word "this," we see what we see *with Maud's own eyes.*

I call Hayden's "too" and Brooks's "this" *voltic* words to evoke association with *volt* and *volta*. *Volt* names a quantity of electrical charge, and I hope by echoing it to suggest that the voltic word carries a charge: it contains more of the information relevant to a poem than a "normal" word contains. *Volta* names the turn in thought that occurs at the transition from octave to sestet in a Petrarchan sonnet, or, more broadly, the analogous turn in a poem whatever its form; by echoing it, I hope to suggest that the voltic word enforces a turn, and in doing so casts light on the rest of the poem, changing our understanding of the whole. *Volt, volta,* and now *voltic* all derive from the Latin *volvere,* a verb meaning to turn or roll, and the root of many English words, including *revolve, revolt, revolution, evolve, evolution, involve, devolve, volte-face, volute, wallow,* and *volume.* The poem turns on (is organized around) the voltic word, and the voltic word turns on (gives power to) the poem.

The Brooks and Hayden poems reveal the voltic word as an especially robust fulfillment of George Oppen's principle that "all words become strange in the crucial moments." I take Oppen to mean not only that words are made strange by moments that are crucial on their own account, independently of words, but that words, strangeness, cruxes, and moments interrelate, inextricably. As the word is made strange by the moment, so is the moment made crucial by the strangeness of the word. The voltic word charges and is charged, turns and is turned. The voltic word is strange, and the moment it marks is crucial. The voltic word is the opposite of a moral, which reiterates in normalizing terms the rest of the work. The moral familiarizes, but the voltic word defamiliarizes, *changing* the rest of the work rather than *reiterating* it, and into *ab*normalizing rather than normalizing terms. Voltic words resemble the "logical operators" of propositional logic in organizing the rest of the locution. If we invented a protocol for formalizing poems, as logicians have invented a protocol for formalizing propositions, Hayden's "too" would merit its own symbol, just as "and" does when the complex proposition "Anna walked and Zuma ran" is formalized as "p · q."

If Lyn Hejinian is right to register the language of poetry *not* as "the language of a genre" but instead as "a language of inquiry," then it may be a strength rather than a weakness of a craft concept for it to impose an attitude of asking, by posing more questions than it answers. The voltic word, I suggest, poses at least the following questions.

Does every poem contain a voltic word? From my two prototypes, does it follow that *every* poem has a voltic word? Surely the list of voltic words could be extended: "Therefore" in James Wright's "Autumn Begins in Martins Ferry, Ohio"; the second "Aloud" in Edna St. Vincent Millay's "If I Should Learn"; "again" in Emily Dickinson's "The Bustle in a House" (1078); "even" in the fourth of Countee Cullen's "Four Epitaphs"; and so on. Still, even if the list of voltic words is long and easy to extend, that does not establish that *every* poem does, or that every poem should, contain a voltic word. The list of poems with end rhyme, too, is long and easy to extend, but it does not follow that every poem does, or should, employ end rhyme.

Is the voltic word genre-specific? My prototypes of the voltic word both occur in poems, and I framed the preceding question in terms of poetry. But can prose, too, employ voltic words? For example, is "down" in this paragraph from Yvonne Vera's novel *Butterfly Burning* a voltic word?

> She wondered but dared not ask. She wanted the two months to pass, quickly, so that she could move into the hospital hostel and start her training and be finished by the end of 1950, but while thinking of that and avoiding her eyes and tolerating his angry touch, she wondered how he knew, and when. The glass on the window held his fingerprints all over it. She wanted to clean the glass, but instead let it remain like that for days. She did not want to interfere with anything he had done. She dared not provoke him. They now lived in a stunning, shattering silence. She could not ask him the questions she wanted answered, so she let it be. If he could not talk about it she would not, but at the back of her mind she wanted desperately to know about his knowing, the extent and breadth of it, and if he too was holding his breath down like she was.

The "down" definitely pushes the sentence away from cliché. We are accustomed to seeing the holding of breath as a figure for tense waiting: "I held my breath in anticipation of his appearance," we say, and "don't hold your breath," "the crowd held its breath when the heroine swooned," and so on. We are *not* accustomed to holding the breath *down* as a figure. The "down" reorients the whole sentence, replacing the customary structuring contrast of inside/outside (one holds one's breath *in*) with the contrast high/low. Which also transforms the kind of concealment being performed in the paragraph, from *containing* to *covering*.

Is the voltic word a character-conferring feature? In Vera's novel, the prose is so elegant that the paragraphs read as prose poems, but is it only in "lyrical" novels that voltic words occur? The presence of voltic words in Vera would lead me to expect them in *Housekeeping* and *The House of Breath*, but should it lead me to expect them in fiction made of flatter prose?

To intensify the question, is it the occurrence in them of voltic words that *makes* lyrical novels lyrical? This question appears with particular force in relation to translation. If the presence of voltic words can characterize a body of prose, is it susceptible to translation from one language to another? The voltic word's "volticity" appears to be more connotative than denotative, so it seems unlikely that the target language will offer a word than can charge and turn the translated work as the voltic word does the original. From which it would follow that the voltic word would be among the things lost in translation, and the voltic-word-enriched work would be untranslatable.

At what scale does the voltic word operate? In both of my prototypes, the entire work, a lyric poem, is very brief. "Those Winter Sundays" is 97 words long, and "Sadie and Maud" 93. The single paragraph just quoted from *Butterfly Burning* is 164 words long. So: do voltic words occur at poem/paragraph scale, a scale of one voltic word per hundred "normal" words, give or take? Or do voltic words occur at a rate of one per *work*, so that there might be one in a poem, though the poem be quite short, and one in a whole novel, though the novel be quite long? To extend the example of *Butterfly Burning*, if I began to search in it for voltic words, might I reasonably expect to find one in each paragraph, or will I find at most a single voltic word in the whole book?

Is being voltic a difference of degree or a difference of kind? Is it that "too" and "this" are wholly voltic, and none of the other words in "Those Winter Sundays" and "Sadie and Maud" are voltic at all, or that all the words in the Hayden and Brooks poems are voltic, and "too" and "this" are just *especially* voltic, *more* voltic than the other words? A different way to ask this would be to ask whether *all* words are voltic. Such ideals as "the right words in the right order," "make every word count," and "le mot juste" seem to apply to all the words in a work, so if the charging and turning that voltic words perform is a good thing for words to do, then it might be plausible to suppose that *every* word should perform such charging and turning, at least to some degree.

Is a word's being voltic distinct from its fulfilling other literary ideals? I might observe, for instance, that the voltic word seems to be especially *efficient*: its having a charge and its turning the poem mean that it is doing a lot of work in a little space. But does that mean that the voltic word is just a particularly visible fulfillment of Chekhov's gun, of ensuring that even a seemingly small detail (in this case a lexical detail) has importance to the whole work? Or is the voltic word an especially clean shave with Occam's razor, a way of making sure that nothing extraneous appears in the work, that everything that needs doing in the work is done with as few doers as possible?

Though my sense for it is made of more questions than answers, I do assert of the voltic word that it embodies this principle of value: *everything belongs, anything that has being has it whole, and nothing can be replaced.* As "hiss" and "moo" are onomatopoetic, *doing* what they refer to, so are voltic words metaphysicopoetic, realizing what they mean. The voltic word operates in lexical enactment of Blake's recommendation "To see a World in a Grain of Sand / And a Heaven in a Wild Flower / Hold Infinity in the palm of your hand / And Eternity in an hour." It achieves the unifying moment that Led Zeppelin's rock anthem urges us toward, the moment "when all are one and one is all." And it contests the limitless fungibility enforced by laissez-faire capitalism (its substitution of price for value, with the consequence that *everything* has a monetary price, that through the medium of currency *anything* can be exchanged for anything else). The voltic word performs with particular intensity, that is to say, the act of resistance that, in 1.1 above, I connected with formulations by Jan Zwicky and Wysława Szymborska. I say here of the voltic word what I said there of the poem in general, that it fulfills the ideal Jan Zwicky names "ontological attention" and describes as "a response to particularity: *this* porch, *this* laundry basket, *this* day," a recalling to ourselves that an "object cannot be substituted for, even when it is an object of considerable generality ('the country', 'cheese', 'garage sales')." And enacts the recognition Szymborska invites us to, that "nothing is usual or normal. Not a single stone and not a single cloud above it. Not a single day and not a single night after it. And above all, not a single existence, not anyone's existence in this world."

Article 10:
Not yet as it should be, no longer as it was.

10.1: Poetry For Dissent

Though its subject is contemporary lyric poetry, Philip Metres' *Behind the Lines* begins with an observation about that ancient paradigm of the epic, Homer's *Iliad*. Metres notes that Thersites, the "only voice of dissent" in the *Iliad*, is "dispensed with quickly," abused both verbally and physically by Odysseus, "much to the delight of the other soldiers" and, Homer assumes, to the delight of the poem's audience. One key element Metres identifies in war poetry, "the absence or ridicule of dissenting voices," also characterizes national epics (such as the *Iliad* for the Greeks, the *Aeneid* for Rome, *Beowulf* for Britain, even the *Kalevala* for so apparently peaceful a people as the Finns). Typically, a national epic is a war poem whose protagonist represents the people because of his prowess in battle. National epics become national epics less because they are belletristic than because they are bellicose; they seldom grant space to dissenting values. All the more interesting, then, that the "great American novel," *Moby Dick*, the closest thing the U.S. has to a national epic, can be viewed (as the *Iliad*, for instance, *cannot* plausibly be viewed) as a narrative of dissent, spoken entirely by a dissenting voice, one who asks us to call him Ishmael, the name of a dissenting voice from the Torah, but could have urged us just as well to call him Thersites.

Eric Havelock (also speaking of Homeric epic) reminds us that war brings out "the essential mechanisms of a culture complex." In an oral society such as the one in and for which the *Iliad* was composed, the epic was "a necessity for government and not just a means for recreation," which entailed that the epic poet "exercise a degree of cultural control over his community which is scarcely imaginable" today. "His epic language would constitute a kind of culture language, a frame of reference and a standard of expression to which in varying degree all members of the community were drawn." If Havelock is right, then the stance toward war that Metres criticizes is a tendency of the genre: epic, "in order to do its job for the community and offer an effective paradigm of social law and custom, must deal with those acts which are conspicuous and political," and with actors of the type we call heroes. Which makes "the heroic paradigm... not romantic but functional and technical." In consequence, epic will be conservative, depicting a myth of origins that rationalizes and validates the status quo. It will depict an original victory of the values and identity that "we" (whoever is included in the presumed audience) most transparently share in common, in preference to the values and identity affirmed by dissent, namely either those that we share in common but not transparently, or those that we do not share in common but (purportedly) ought to.

The propensity of national epics toward conservatism should not surprise us, since the role of epic in constructing culture, language, and custom, is complemented and magnified by the dynamics of literary reception and preservation. The voices of those empowered by a state are more likely to be heard, valued, and preserved than are the voices of that state's poor and disenfranchised, and those empowered by a state have the greatest stake in that state's legitimation. Those who benefit most from existing social organization will be those most authorized to tell stories, and also best able to preserve and disseminate the stories they prefer. As Thomas R. Hietala points out, "critics of national policy seldom reach generations other than their own, for history... often records only the dominant voices of the past." That combination — epic's role in shaping culture, and the dynamics of literary preservation — means that the conservatism of national epics in general should not surprise us, but also means that the dissenting voice of Moby Dick should.

Moby Dick, published in 1851, appeared at the height of expansionist fervor in the United States. In 1840 the United States covered approximately one quarter of the geographical area it covers today, but, Frederick Merk points out, in the 1840s "a form of expansionism novel in name, appeal, and theory made its appearance." That form of expansionism took the name "manifest destiny," and "attracted enough persons by the mid-1840's to constitute a movement." John L. O'Sullivan coined the term in 1845, and his disdain for other nations' dissent resembles Odysseus' disdain for Thersites' dissent in the *Iliad*: other nations, O'Sullivan contends, have interfered with annexation "for the avowed object of thwarting our policy and hampering our power, limiting our greatness and checking the fulfilment of our manifest destiny to overspread the continent allotted by Providence for the free development of our yearly multiplying millions."

Manifest destiny is, in Hietala's words, a "legitimizing myth of empire" that justifies American expansion and "implicitly sanction[s] the dispossession of all non-Anglo peoples on the continent." To legitimate dispossession, though, would-be dispossessers must dehumanize those to be dispossessed. To make it plausible that a just God would decree that land be taken from "them" and awarded to "us," "we" must be fully human, and "they" must not be. In this regard, Melville's Ishmael takes Thersites' role, articulating an oppositional stance, dissenting from the legitimizing myth and its premises. Ishmael repeatedly starts with a dehumanizing view of the non-Anglo other, but after an edifying encounter with that other comes to revise his original view, recognizing the other's humanity. Melville's Ishmael is more subtle and articulate than Homer's Thersites, but he still dissents: he "shouts down" the dismissal of the non-Anglo other on which depends the legitimizing myth Melville's contemporaries called manifest destiny.

Queequeg occasions many of Ishmael's recognitions. In their first encounter, Ishmael's recognition of Queequeg's humanity follows the pattern *Moby Dick*'s readers soon come to recognize. The Spouter-Inn in New Bedford, where Ishmael has stopped on his way to Nantucket, does not have a room available, so he is asked by the innkeeper, "'you haint no objections to sharing a harpooneer's blanket, have ye?'" Ishmael reluctantly agrees, but then his fears begin to mount. The innkeeper manipulates those fears, warning Ishmael that "'the harpooneer is a dark complexioned chap'" who "eats nothing but steaks, and likes 'em rare," characteristics that lead Ishmael to want to know from the innkeeper "who and what this harpooneer is, and whether I shall be in all respects safe" in the room with him. Ishmael concludes, after being told that the harpooneer is late returning to the inn because he is out trying to sell a shrunken head, that "that harpooneer is a dangerous man," and is only reassured by the innkeeper that the bed is big, not that the harpooneer is civil. Ishmael agrees to share a bed with the harpooneer, but his first sight confirms his fears: "good heavens! what a sight! Such a face! It was of a dark, purplish, yellow color, here and there stuck over with large, blackish looking squares. Yes, it's just as I thought, he's a terrible bedfellow." He looks different from me; ergo, he must pose a threat.

Once Ishmael is *interacting with* and not only *observing* Queequeg, though, he immediately recognizes Queequeg's civility. Queequeg responds calmly when the innkeeper informs him that he will be sharing his bed with Ishmael. He motions for Ishmael to get in bed, and Ishmael concedes, "He really did this in not only a civil but a really kind and charitable way." Further reflection leads Ishmael to conclude, "the man's a human being just as I am: he has just as much reason to fear me, as I have to be afraid of him. Better sleep with a sober cannibal than a drunken Christian." The pattern is established: encouraged by the prejudices of his fellow Anglos, Ishmael will initially regard non-Anglos with prejudice, but then after interaction with the person in question, Ishmael will come to recognize and acknowledge that person's humanity.

This type of recognition in *Moby Dick* differs from the anagnorisis of Greek tragedy, in which the recognition occurs too late to stop the fatal results, but occurs in the protagonist whose hubris brings about the tragic fall. The recognition in *Oedipus* occurs late, and in Oedipus himself. In *Moby Dick*, the recognition occurs early, but occurs in the speaker, whose role is much more like that of the Greek chorus than of the protagonist. It is Ishmael, not Ahab, who recognizes humanity in other humans (though it would be ecocritically, posthumanistically interesting to consider in this light Ahab's recognizing humanity in the whale). Ishmael's pattern of coming to recognize the humanity in non-Anglo others, and thus of portraying them as fully human despite their treatment by others, is repeated throughout: in the three harpooneers, in the old cook, in Pip.

Although the term "manifest destiny" is used with less frequency today, we still stand in need of the recognition *Moby Dick* provides. That recognition was timely, but is also timeless, posing a challenge not only to such of its predecessors as Homer but also to legitimizing myths as they embed themselves in culture today. By encapsulating the sense that "it was manifest or evident that the United States was destined to expand 'from sea to shining sea,'" the concept of manifest destiny, Mark S. Joy observes, "portrayed America's expansion in terms of destiny and fate," offering a "mythic interpretation of American expansion" that "remains widely popular," even if the term is invoked less often and even though "the facts simply do not support it." The same elements that compose the concept of manifest destiny still have popular appeal: they were foregrounded, for instance, in the legitimizing myth invoked by George W. Bush in his statements leading up to the 2003 American invasion of Iraq. I will cite only one such speech as representative; in it Bush appeals to destiny, for instance: "I'm going to take our time to make sure we get the policy right, no matter what part of the world we're in. But I understand that freedom has called us into action — I mean, history has called us into action to defend freedom. I understand where we stand now in history. We have an obligation to the future. And this great country will not shirk its obligation." He depicts the full human-ity of "us": "You need to know there's a lot of people working a lot of hours to protect us. A lot of good folks that work in the federal government..., doing everything they can to chase down every possible lead, every hint that somebody might be fixing to do something to the American people." He also depicts "them" as less than fully human: "And they're out there. The killers are out there. And that's all they are, by the way. They are nothing but a bunch of cold-blooded killers, who hate America because we love freedom. They hate us because we love the values of freedom of religion, freedom to speak, freedom to campaign the way you want to, freedom to assemble. They can't stand that." We must fulfil the divine purpose on earth by imposing ourselves on an ever wider area, without clear boundaries: "I believe we can achieve peace by being strong and determined in parts of the world where peace seems to be far away. I believe we can achieve peace in the Middle East. I believe we can achieve peace in South Asia. I believe this great nation, by being strong and determined and standing on prin-ciples and adhering to our universal values, can help the world achieve peace." As with an appeal to manifest destiny per se, Bush's appeal envi-sions peace as occurring not through reconciliation with an other regarded as one's equal, but through expansion into the other's domain, subduing or eliminating an other regarded as less than human, managing people and places that cannot manage without us.

Moby Dick dissents from this approach. Ishmael repeatedly alters his own understanding when confronted with a non-Anglo other, coming to recognize that other as fully competent and fully human. Given the long and firmly established tradition in national epics of excluding dissent, such embrace of dissent is surprising in "the Great American Novel." For those of us who esteem Thersites' point of view at least as much as Achilles' point of view, who find dissent at least as patriotic a posture as jingoism, this aspect of *Moby Dick*, its acknowledgment of the non-Anglo other and its questioning of the most prevalent legitimizing myth of empire, is much to be valued.

10.2: Poetry For Hybridity

Robert Bringhurst describes myths as "doorways between realms," a description he amplifies by placing the "journey between worlds" among "the most basic mythic themes. Gilgamesh, Persephone, Eurydike and Orpheus, Odysseus, Cuchulain, Christ, Mohammed, Satan, God and countless other... creatures of the mythworld make such visitations," sometimes with "no other role to play, no other duty to perform, except to make these journeys that connect and yet keep separate the worlds within the world." Bringhurst's observation notes the persistence across time and across cultures of a metaphor for simultaneously connecting and separating worlds. Bringhurst gives the journey, i.e. trans*location*, as his example of a doorway between realms, but trans*formation* also serves as such a doorway, connecting and yet keeping separate "the worlds within the world," and the being within the being.

As a literary and cultural vehicle for understanding humanity, transformation functions the way caricature functions, by greatly exaggerating a given feature as a way of focusing attention on it. As a figure for transformation, metamorphosis has been, as the journey has been for translocation, persistent across time. The metamorphosis, typically transformation of an animal into a human or vice versa, has been one of the most frequent and perduring tropes in literature: Ovid and Kafka offer especially familiar examples. But the very persistence of the metaphor makes all the more surprising a sudden preference for another figure of transformation. If metamorphosis has been for centuries the preferred figure for transformation, then a sudden change would seem to mark a cultural shift of some magnitude. It suggests that we understand humanity in a way that differs fundamentally from past usage and understanding.

That there has been just such a dramatic change, namely that hybridity is now employed more often as a figure of transformation than is metamorphosis, can be vividly depicted by means of Google's Ngram Viewer, a function that scans the vast corpus of books now digitized by Google, and presents a chart tracking frequency of usage of the search term(s) in that corpus.

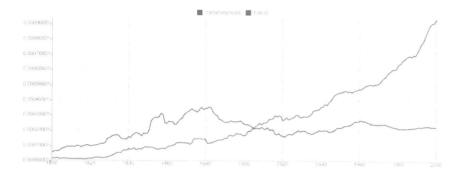

The graph above charts the relative frequency of the terms "metamorpho-sis" and "hybrid." It shows "metamorphosis" rising to its most frequent usage around 1880, then leveling off around 1900 to a fairly constant level of usage from 1900 to 2000. "Hybrid" increases gradually from 1800 on, beginning with a lower frequency of usage than that of "metamorphosis" but equaling it around 1900, and continuing to increase, with a surge from about 1970 through the end of the graph, so that in 2000 "hybrid" is used five times as often as "metamorphosis." By this measure, "metamorphosis" is used in 2000 with approximately the same frequency as in 1850, but "hybrid" is used in 2000 approximately ten times as often as it was in 1850.

In light of such a trend, it is worth asking ourselves: What is distinctive about the figure of hybridity? Is the recent surge of interest in hybridity justified? Does hybridity matter? They are questions of the sort I would call "insistent" — not susceptible to definitive answer, but of pressing con-cern to humans — so I will not purport to *answer* them conclusively, only to *pose* them in ways that may be provocative and fruitful, that may suggest avenues for further inquiry.

What is distinctive about the figure of hybridity? The contemporary preoccupation with hybridity reflects a shift in the circumstances and con-cerns of humanity. The cultural shifts marked by the dramatic change in the relative frequency of their usage can be more readily identified after explicit comparison of the terms themselves.

When Proteus metamorphoses into a tiger, he mutates into the tiger; the hybrid Pan, in contrast, merges human with goat. In a metamorpho-sis, then, one form replaces another; but altogether only two forms are involved. In a hybrid, two forms join to create a form that is neither the one nor the other; so three forms are involved or implied. Metamorphosis is a substitution of one form for another, hybridity a combination of one form with another. Ultimately things are not quite so simple, nor the distinction quite so clean. For example, when Proteus metamorphoses into the tiger, his outward form has changed, but his inward identity has not: he retains a continuous intention throughout his changes (e.g. to escape Odysseus' hold), and he retains continuous powers (tigers can't change form, only Proteus can), so it is only one *form* that replaces another form, not a whole being that replaces another whole being. But the distinction need not be "clean" to be functional.

A metamorphosis is an event: yesterday I was an office clerk, this morning I am a giant beetle. Hybridity is an ongoing, continuous condition: my cyborgness persists. The two are related: metamorphosis results, of course, in a condition, but the metamorphosis itself is the event of transformation; hybridity may result from an event, but the hybridity is the condition brought about by the transformation, not the event of transformation. Moreover, the condition in which metamorphosis results is not the condition of hybridity; I was an office clerk, now I'm another thing altogether. The new condition is discontinuous with the old; I am an office clerk no longer. Similarly, the condition of hybridity does not result from the event of metamorphosis; I may have been born a cyborg or may have made myself into one later, but I didn't metamorphose into one.

A metamorphosis most often happens suddenly; I wake up one morning, and I'm a cockroach. Hybridity more often occurs gradually; we didn't realize how much a part of ourselves our technology had become until one of us couldn't articulate his research in a conference session because he couldn't call up the file on the available computer. We saw computers as accidental, as tools we could use or not, at will. His, though, proved itself essential, a part of his identity; he was not the same scholar without it. Metamorphosis, as an event, seems more often reversible; hybridity, as a condition, seems more persistent. Proteus can just change back into himself; returning to the days of the typewriter and mimeograph looks more complicated. Metamorphosis is a complete transformation, in the sense that one form becomes another; all the elements of one form are replaced by all the elements of another. It is momentous: it occurs — begins and ends — at a point in time. Hybridity is a partial transformation, in the sense that some but not all elements of one form join with some but not all elements of another form; neither originating form is present in its entirety, and neither is entirely absent. It has duration: it is ongoing, with a beginning and ending that are distant from one another and that may appear as horizons rather than as points.

The spatiality of the two types of transformation correlates with their temporality. In metamorphosis the system (me, or humanity) is breached by the environment. I had maintained borders that kept me distinct from my environment, but it broke through when I became a cockroach; I became (part of) my environment, no longer distinct from it. The distinctness of my particular system from others, my humanity as that which permits me to move *through* nature and look *out* at it, is lost. Thus, metamorphosis occurs as an event: I had a quality but lost it. In hybridity, the border between system and environment is not breached, it's just not clear where it is or whether there is a border. If I'm part human and part wolf, am I part of "nature" or not? My humanity as that which permits me to move *through* nature and look *out* at it, is compromised. Thus, hybridity occurs as a condition rather than as an event: it is not that the border between system and environment has been breached at some point, but that as an ongoing condition the border, insofar as there is one at all, is porous or unmarked.

The transformations respond to different perceived threats to humankind. Where the greatest threat to humanity is magic, that which resists explanation and evades prediction, metamorphosis will figure the human condition well. If I don't know what will happen next, nothing ensures that I will not suddenly be transformed into a laurel tree or a giant beetle, or that no god metamorphosed into a swan will rape me. I must be wary of inexplicable and unpredictable surprise. Change appears as *intervention*. In contrast, if what threatens me most immediately is not the magical but the inevitable, that the causes of which I may recognize but cannot manipulate, then hybridity will be the more apt figure for the human condition. An unmanageable swell of digital technology will threaten to transform me into a cyborg moving through artificial environments (auto to airport terminal to airplane) with my bluetooth in my ear and my boarding pass on my iPhone. Change appears as *momentum*. I can see it coming, I just can't stop it.

I depend on the permanency and uniformity of the laws of nature: to navigate safely and successfully through my life, I need the gravity that was there yesterday still to be there tomorrow. That permanency and uniformity, though, is what metamorphosis threatens. I need to be able to count on waking up as a human tomorrow just like I did this morning, but metamorphosis says I might not. Hybridity, in contrast, threatens human exceptionalism. In innumerable ways I act as if humans were distinguished from other things in nature. Different candidates for what distinguishes us have been offered: our capacity for language, our capacity for reason, and so on. Whatever the particular distinction, though, I need for there to *be* a distinction: I kill dandelions without remorse, but I account the killing of humans unjust; I own a dog and force her to wear a collar at all times, but I account ownership and collaring of humans unjust. Only on the basis of exceptionalism can I maintain these contrasting behaviors. But hybridity threatens that exceptionalism: if I can be part machine and part human, or part wolf and part human, then the human part doesn't look so exceptional after all.

In *A Grammar of Motives*, after identifying what he calls "the pentad" (act, scene, agent, agency, purpose), Kenneth Burke notes a number of "ratios" (correspondences between elements) that operate in literature and other forms of discourse. Burke defines very simply the terms relevant here: act is "what took place, in thought or deed"; scene is "the background of the act, the situation in which it occurred"; and agent is "what person or kind of person... performed the act." The "ratios" are "principles of determination." So the act-agent ratio posits a relationship between what is done and who does it. My suggestion here is that metamorphosis concerns itself primarily with that ratio. It asks how who I am relates to what I do. What would I do, how would I live, if I were a giant cockroach? Hybridity, in contrast, concerns itself primarily, I suggest, with the scene-agent ratio; that is, it asks how who I am relates to my surroundings. If I am a cyborg, my standing in and connection to the environment in which I exist will be different than they will be if I am a human. Explicit correlation can be made between these ratios and the endangered sources of security. If what is threatened is the permanency and uniformity of the laws of nature, then the questions "*What must I do* (act) to ward off the unpredictable?" and "*Who must I be* (agent) to ward it off?" will be equivalents. If instead human exceptionalism is the threatened source of security, the most pertinent question will be "What limits do my surroundings (scene) impose on me (agent)?"

Metamorphosis depicts a need for propitiation. The agency being propitiated need not be a personified deity, but whatever is behind the environment's effects on me, I want some way of warding off those effects. The environment is bigger and stronger than I am, capable at any moment of harming me: I might be struck by lightning, say, or swept off in a flash flood. Against such dangers, I cannot defend myself effectively; I am subject to sudden and radical transformation. Hybridity addresses a need for sustainability, that is for mitigating our own effects on the environment. I must become different, effect a unity with the environment, to ensure that my own actions do not come back to haunt me. The danger, in other words, is less that the environment will act against me capriciously than that I will act in violation of nature's inexorability.

A different kind of agency is appropriate to each term. In a world in which metamorphosis occurs, or in which it is perceived as a possibility or a threat, the agency would be one that intervenes, that creates events, that can surprise. What we face is the irresistible force. Though the agency need not be personified, if it *were* personified, it would be personified as a god, i.e. as an agency outside of, or above, or before conditions themselves. The source of the caprice, the threat of surprise, occurs in the gap between conditions and agency. Something other than, and ontologically prior to, the conditions themselves *shapes* the conditions: the crops were parched, but God sent us rain. Agency in a world of hybridity, a world of conditions rather than events, would be the sort we name, and personify as, Nature (with a capital N). What we face is the immovable object. I.e., there is no gap between conditions and agency: nothing outside of conditions acts on them or through them. Conditions express only themselves; what conditions *do* is what conditions *are*. Consequently, though agency need not be personified in this case any more than in the other, if it *is* personified, what is personified is the whole of the conditions themselves. In the world of metamorphosis, transcendence arises from the fact that I experience conditions, but something (that I can experience only through or as the conditions) supervenes upon the conditions. To see sub specie aeternitatis would be to see from the point of view of agency rather than of the conditions, to be above conditions rather than within them. In the world of hybridity, transcendence arises from the fact that I experience only part of the conditions, not the whole of the conditions. I see the blue sky overhead, but not the storm clouds gathering a hundred miles west. To see sub specie aeternitatis would be to see all of the conditions at once, not only a part of them.

In a world of metamorphosis, it is nature that needs to be regulated, moderated, checked, controlled. What I want is for the god to be pleased or distracted, the active forces mollified, so that they do not act on me, do not produce the event of metamorphosis that makes me into something other than myself. In a world of hybridity, nothing saves me from myself; instead of the external world threatening to overwhelm me, I (we, humanity) threaten to overwhelm it. Now that we are mechanical/digital cyborgs, the events to forestall are those (such as oil spills) that follow from our condition, but are ultimately not only destructive of other things but also *self*-destructive.

Is the recent surge of interest in hybridity justified? Unprecedented levels of violence in the twentieth and twenty-first centuries (world wars, genocides, terrorist acts), combined with such scientific developments as the sequencing of the genome, demand ongoing reconsideration of humanity in all spheres. In philosophy and cultural studies, hybridity and the cyborg and the posthuman all have gained currency as ways of undertaking such reconsideration.

An intellectual and theoretical movement that gets labeled, or labels itself, with a moniker employing the prefix "post-" (poststructuralism, postmodernism, postcolonialism...) will depend for its rationale on some version of the claim that "Things are different now." Resistance to the movement will depend on the contrary claim, "No, they're not." Dialogue between proponents and opponents of the "post-" theory itself has no hope of progressing until some common ground has been established about whether or not things are relevantly different, and if so in what ways. You and I will not be able to agree on whether a theory is adequate to conditions (whether, in other words, it describes them aptly, or guides us wisely through them) until we share some sense about what the conditions *are* to which the theory is being adequated.

The "things" that are (or are not) different now might be facts them-selves, or they might be our understanding of or access to the facts. That understanding might stand in reciprocal relation to the new theory; that is, we might see the facts in a new light because we have the theory, and see the theory as sound because the facts as we now understand them support the theory. So in physics, for example, the facts themselves did not change in the first half of the twentieth century (gravity and acceleration did not suddenly become equivalent, nor did space suddenly start being relative to the observer after having been absolute before), but our understanding of the facts did change, and not independently of the new theory called for by the understanding of the facts. That is, we didn't develop a new un-derstanding of the facts, and then come up with relativity (and quantum) afterward to account for the ways that "things are different now"; our sense that "things are different now" arose along with the theory. Nor need the relationship between newer and older theory be simple substitution. If I'm a researcher investigating neutrinos I'll rely heavily on quantum, and if I'm a NASA engineer calculating the trajectory of a space telescope I'll rely on relativity, but if I'm a poet calculating how fast I'll have to drive to get to Buffalo on time Newtonian mechanics will do just fine.

I contend that things *are* different now, in ways that invite the kinds of inquiry and assertion now clustered under the label "posthumanism," and that, as regards metamorphosis and hybridity, both the facts and our understanding of them give reason to regard hybridity as the more salient figure, though historically metamorphosis has been so regarded. This is not to dismiss metamorphosis altogether, or to treat hybridity as a panacea for our intellectual and cultural problems, nor does it constitute an apology for posthumanism or an exposition of it, only to identify common ground for dialogue, to offer some prolegomena to any future posthumanism.

At least two elements of the human situation seem clearly and demon-strably different now than they were in the past, whether one compares our current situation to a recent past (say, when the most important sing-er was Mick Jagger) or to a distant past (e.g. when the most important singer was Homer). One changed element of the human situation is that there are more of us now. The U.S. Census Bureau estimates that in 10,000 B.C.E. there were between 1 million and 10 million humans on earth; that by 1 C.E. there were between 170 million and 400 million; that by 1900 C.E. there were just over 1.5 billion humans; and that now there are over 7 billion humans. If these estimates are correct, human population has more than quadrupled in the last 110 years. There are more people today in China alone than there were in 1900 on the whole planet. The other changed element is that technology is more pervasive in human experience than ever before. By pervasive I mean both that technology is distributed more widely across the human population than ever before, and that its role in one human life is, on average, more extensive than ever before. This applies both to mechanical and to digital technologies. Of mechanical technologies, regarding their wide distribution, all of us are aware, for example, of the growing number of automobiles in India; and regarding the extensive role of mechanical technologies in individual lives, any of us could reflect on the leaf blowers or cappucino machines we own that our grandparents managed without. Of digital technologies, cell phones alone offer plenty of evidence. Regarding their wide distribution, one need only ask oneself how many people one can name who do *not* own a cell phone; and regarding their extensive role in individual lives, we could note such phenomena as the need to make laws against texting while driving.

Though these two differences suffice by themselves to establish that "things are different now," I suggest that they are representative, that in other words this pairing could be expanded into a lengthy list. Merely observing ways in which these changes are not isolated would extend the list: there are more people on earth, and consequently there is less wilderness; there are more people on earth, so urbanization is increasing; technology is more pervasive, so fuel use is high; and so on.

Does hybridity matter? I have tried to establish three points so far: (1) that hybridity has supplanted metamorphosis as the preferred metaphor for transformation, (2) that hybridity and metamorphosis differ substantially from one another, and (3) that, at least as concerns humans, the world is substantially different now than it has been in the past. Those points together raise a concluding question: Do the differences noted in (2) and (3) correlate in such a way that they motivate (1)? In other words, does hybridity — to appeal again to criteria I employed earlier — describe our conditions more aptly than does metamorphosis? Does it guide us wisely through those conditions?

I believe the answer is yes. When there were one million humans on earth, and none of those humans employed technologies that entailed extraction and burning of fossil fuels, what the world would do to me was the biggest threat to me: the drought that will ruin my harvest, the fire that will consume my dwelling. There aren't enough humans doing enough things with enough collective impact to radically alter the conditions for human survival and flourishing. I know that the drought or fire might come, but I can't see them coming. Because I cannot defend myself effectively against such dangers, because I and what I depend on for survival are subject to sudden and radical transformation, propitiation of whatever is behind the threats is an appropriate response, and to understand transformations as metamorphoses is conceptually sound.

Now that there are nearly seven billion humans on the earth, and rapidly increasing numbers of them are employing, with rapidly increasing frequency, technologies that depend on fossil fuels, what we are doing cannot but have an impact on the conditions needed for our survival. What I need is not to figure out how to avoid "acts of God," but how to mitigate my own — *our* own — effects on the environment, to align with its laws in such a way that my actions do not "come back to bite me." Not what nature will do to me, but what I am doing in nature, now poses the biggest threat to me. An unforeseeable disaster (tsunami, volcanic eruption) might kill thousands of people, but increasing numbers of humans making increased use of technologies that depend on fossil fuels might lead to conditions no longer amenable to the survival of the human species. It is now more urgent that I mitigate my own effects on the environment than that I propitiate whatever gods may be. Effects for which humans are the cause, rather than those for which non-human agency is the cause, are now the greatest danger to humans, so change in human activity is the appropriate response, and hybridity an apt conceptual framework for understanding transformation.

To quote Hélène Cixous, "All our primitive or poetic experiences are either separations or nonseparations: the difficulty of defining the border between sexes, between species, and also between the high and the low." Cixous says that one "who doesn't tremble while crossing a border doesn't know there is a border and doesn't cast doubt on their own definition. The person who trembles while crossing a border casts doubt on their own definition, not only on their passport, not only on their driver's license but also on every aspect and form of their definition.... What 'nature' are we? What 'species' are we?" Metamorphosis and hybridity both represent primitive, poetic experiences; both depict borders, or (in Bringhurst's terms) simultaneously connect and separate worlds, but there is reason to consider hybridity more fruitful now than metamorphosis in answering Cixous's questions, "What 'nature' are we? What 'species' are we?"

Amendments

1.1: It wasn't so hard to learn *what to do*, but here I am, more of my life behind me than up ahead, still trying to sort out *how to be*, asking for help from poetry.

1.2: As a defense against fundamentalism's threat to poetry, too, not only to religion, may I prove ecumenical. Or agnostic.

2.1: More than I mean what I say, I mean what I don't say. I mean to say all I must, but more than that I mean to *not* say all I can.

2.2: I seek to make my voice singular, but not by making it single, not by making it voiced, and not by making it mine.

3.1: I resolved the paradox by forfeiting my quest for resolution. I consoled myself for my instability by repeating the same change again and again.

3.2: I could not see what I saw, or see myself seeing, but I could see *that* I was seeing, and seeing something I wished I could see.

4.1: Neither my thinking nor my doing is stable. In the metastability of the two in tension, poetry intervenes.

4.2: I must revise my life, I know, but first I need to muster the courage to pose myself the questions, answers to which might show me *how* to undertake *what* revisions.

5.1: Language in showing me the world divides me from the world, in showing me myself divides me from myself, in joining me to others divides me from others. Poetry in giving me language divides me from language.

5.2: I recognize my distance from myself in our distance from one another and the distance of the world that might be from the world that is.

6.1: *The* political struggle: who gets to ask what questions of whom. Who must answer, in ways that satisfy whom. War: insistence that I *will* ask and *won't* answer.

6.2: *Do you see what I see?* Poetry asks that question in wonder, violence asks it as a threat.

7.1: If of my life it holds that "in my beginning is my end," then of my singing must it also hold.

7.2: Language becomes mine as water becomes mine, only by swallowing it. I know you're thirsty. Me, too.

8.1: Poetry offers one case in which I support back-conjugating a verb: I don't *proceed* from word to word, but I do *process*.

8.2: Poetry is not my answer to "Who am I?" but it is my way of asking. I don't expect an answer, but I do plan to keep asking.

9.1: In the poem I venture all of me: the whole of me, and the many of me.

9.2: To say differently what I saw is *both* to see differently what I saw, and to see something different.

10.1: Poetry a contrary of manifest destiny: not something to make whatever is before me belong to me, but something to make me belong to whatever is before me.

10.2: If I could ascertain what two worlds I am between, I could better understand what I am, between them.

Works Cited

Preamble

Wittgenstein, Ludwig. *Culture and Value*. Ed. G. H. von Wright. Trans. Peter Winch. U. of Chicago Press, 1980.

Milosz, Czeslaw. "Ars Poetica?" Trans. Milosz and Lillian Vallee. In *New and Collected Poems 1931-2001*. Ecco, 2003. 240-41.

Article 1:
Make another world, make this world otherwise.
1.1: Poetry Against Growth

Bernstein, Charles. *A Poetics*. Harvard U. Press, 1992.

Dine, Janet. "Rigging the Risks: Why commercial law kills." *Irish Pages* 6:1 (2011): 46-63.

Farmer, Paul. *Pathologies of Power: Health, Human Rights, and the New War on the Poor*. U. of California Press, 2003.

Mackey, Louis. *An Ancient Quarrel Continued: The Troubled Marriage of Philosophy and Literature*. U. Press of America, 2002.

Morton, Timothy. *Hyperobjects: Philosophy and Ecology after the End of the World*. U. of Minnesota Press, 2013.

Nussbaum, Martha. *Not for Profit: Why Democracy Needs the Humanities*. Princeton U. Press, 2010.

Szymborska, Wisława. *Poems New and Collected: 1957-1997*. Trans. Stanisław Barańczak and Clare Cavanagh. Harcourt, 1998.

Thoreau, Henry David. *Walden*. Ed. J. Lyndon Shanley. Princeton U. Press, 1989.

Wittgenstein, Ludwig. *Zettel*. Ed. G. E. M. Anscombe and G. H. von Wright. Trans. G. E. M. Anscombe. U. of California Press, 1970.

Zwicky, Jan. *Lyric Philosophy*. U. of Toronto Press, 1992.

----------. *Wisdom & Metaphor*. Gaspereau Press, 2003.

1.2: Poetry Against Poems

Aristotle. *Poetics.* Trans. Ingram Bywater. In *The Basic Works of Aristotle.* Ed. Richard McKeon. Random House, 1941.

Creeley, Robert. *Was That a Real Poem & other essays.* Ed. Donald Allen. Four Seasons Foundation, 1978.

Cunningham, J. V. *The Collected Essays of J. V. Cunningham.* Swallow Press, 1976.

Fishman, Lisa. *Flower Cart.* Ahsahta Press, 2011.

----------. "An author's statement." http://ahsahtapress.boisestate.edu/books/fishman3/fishman3-author.htm

Lakoff, George. *Women, Fire, and Dangerous Things: What Categories Reveal about the Mind.* U. of Chicago Press, 1987.

Osman, Jena. *The Network.* Fence Books, 2011.

Rankine, Claudia. *Don't Let Me Be Lonely.* Graywolf Press, 2004.

Sen, Amartya. *The Idea of Justice.* Harvard U. Press, 2009.

----------. *On Ethics and Economics.* Basil Blackwell, 1987.

Shakespeare, William. *The Riverside Shakespeare.* Houghton Mifflin, 1974.

Zwicky, Jan. *Lyric Philosophy.* U. of Toronto Press, 1992.

Article 2:

Double stance, double vision.

2.1: Poetry For Relationship

Bishop, Elizabeth. *The Complete Poems 1927-1979.* Farrar Straus Giroux, 1983.

Empson, William. *Seven Types of Ambiguity.* 2nd ed. New Directions, 1947.

McFall, Lynne. *Happiness.* Peter Lang, 1989.

Wittgenstein, Ludwig. *Tractatus Logico-Philosophicus.* Trans. D. F. Pears and B. F. McGuinness. Routledge, 1961.

2.2: Poetry For Justice

Brooks, Gwendolyn. *Selected Poems.* Harper Perennial, 1963.

Lorde, Audre. *Sister Outsider: Essays and Speeches.* Crossing Press, 1984.

Nussbaum, Martha C. *Poetic Justice: The Literary Imagination and Public Life*. Beacon Press, 1995.

Rich, Adrienne. *What Is Found There: Notebooks on Poetry and Politics*. W. W. Norton, 1993.

Sen, Amartya. *The Idea of Justice*. Harvard U. Press, 2009.

Smith, Adam. *The Theory of Moral Sentiments*. Garland, 1971.

Wood, James. *How Fiction Works*. Farrar, Straus and Giroux, 2009.

Article 3:
Think making, make thinking.

3.1: Poetry Against Philosophy

Bruns, Gerald L. *The Material of Poetry: Sketches for a Philosophical Poetics*. U. of Georgia Press, 2005.

Bernstein, Charles. *My Way: Speeches and Poems*. U. of Chicago Press, 1999.

Hejinian, Lyn. *The Language of Inquiry*. U. of California Press, 2000.

Hobbes, Thomas. *Leviathan*. Ed. C. B. Macpherson. Penguin, 1968.

Mackey, Louis. *An Ancient Quarrel Continued: The Troubled Marriage of Philosophy and Literature*. U. Press of America, 2002.

----------. *Fact, Fiction, and Representation: Four Novels by Gilbert Sorrentino*. Camden House, 1997.

----------. *Kierkegaard: A Kind of Poet*. U. of Pennsylvania Press, 1971.

----------. *Points of View: Readings of Kierkegaard*. Florida State U. Press, 1986.

Scalapino, Leslie. *The Public World / Syntactically Impermanence*. Wesleyan U. Press, 1999.

3.2: Poetry Against Fragmentation

Glissant, Édouard. *Poetic Intention*. Trans. Nathalie Stephens with Anne Malena. Nightboat Books, 2010.

Kahn, Charles H. *The Art and Thought of Heraclitus*. Cambridge U. Press, 1979.

Kelsey, Karla. "Lineation in the Land of the New Sentence." In *A Broken Thing: Poets on the Line*. Ed. Emily Rosko and Anton Vander Zee. U. of Iowa Press, 2011. 138-41.

Kirk, G. S. and J. E. Raven. *The Presocratic Philosophers: A Critical History with a Selection of Texts.* Cambridge U. Press, 1957.

Luhmann, Niklas. *Art as a Social System.* Trans. Eva M. Knodt. Stanford U. Press, 2000.

Warren, James. *Presocratics: Natural Philosophers before Socrates.* U. of California Press, 2007.

Zwicky, Jan. "Oracularity." *Metaphilosophy* 34:3 (July 2003): 488-509.

Article 4:

See what is at stake, change what is at stake.

4.1: Poetry for Reparation

Aravamudan, Srinivas. *Tropicopolitans: Colonialism and Agency, 1688-1804.* Duke U. Press, 1999.

Hayden, Robert. "Frederick Douglass." In *Collected Poems.* Ed. Frederick Glaysher. Liveright, 1985.

Merwin, W. S. *The Folding Cliffs.* Alfred A. Knopf, 1998.

Schneider, Wendie Ellen. "Merchants and the Creation of a Westernized Judiciary in Hawai'i." *The Yale Law Journal* 108:6 (April 1999). 1389-1424.

Žižek, Slavoj. *The Parallax View.* MIT Press, 2006.

4.2: Poetry for Preparation

Badiou, Alain. *Second Manifesto for Philosophy.* Trans. Louise Burchill. Polity Press, 2011.

Burt, John. "W. S. Merwin's *The Folding Cliffs.*" *Raritan* 19:3 (Winter 2000): 115-34.

Kirsch, Adam. "The Poet's Plague." *The New Republic* 220:12 (22 March 1999): 40-45.

Mackey, Louis. *Faith Order Understanding: Natural Theology in the Augustinian Tradition.* Pontifical Institute of Mediaeval Studies, 2011.

Merwin, W. S. *The Folding Cliffs.* Alfred A. Knopf, 1998.

Milton, John. *Complete Poems and Major Prose.* Ed. Merritt Y. Hughes. The Odyssey Press, 1957.

Shakespeare, William. *The Riverside Shakespeare.* Houghton Mifflin, 1974.

Thurston, Michael. "The Substance of the Island: W. S. Merwin's Lyrical Epic." *Kenyon Review* 22:3/4 (Summer/Fall 2000): 180-86.

Wordsworth, William. *The Poetical Works of Wordsworth*. Ed. Thomas Hutchinson. Oxford U. Press, 1932.

Article 5:
Everything that descends must diverge.
5.1: Poetry Against Patriarchy

Aristotle. *Poetics*. Trans. Ingram Bywater. In *The Basic Works of Aristotle*, ed. Richard McKeon. Random House, 1941.

Cooke, Miriam. *Women and the War Story*. U. of California Press, 1996.

Notley, Alice. *The Descent of Alette*. Penguin, 1996.

----------. *Grave of Light: New and Selected Poems 1970-2005*. Wesleyan U. Press, 2006.

5.2: Poetry Against Tyranny

Cassell, Anthony K. *Dante's Fearful Art of Justice*. U. of Toronto Press, 1984.

Dante. *The Inferno*. Trans. Robert Pinsky. Farrar, Straus and Giroux, 1994.

Frankfurt, Harry G. "Freedom of the Will and the Concept of a Person." *The Journal of Philosophy* 68:1 (14 January 1971): 5-20.

Kateb, George. *Patriotism and Other Mistakes*. Yale U. Press, 2006.

Notley, Alice. *The Descent of Alette*. Penguin, 1996.

----------. "Women and Poetry." In *Coming After: Essays on Poetry*. U. of Michigan Press, 2005. 167-70.

Plato. *Republic*. Trans. G. M. A. Grube, revised by C. D. C. Reeve. In *Plato: Complete Works*. Ed. John M. Cooper. Hackett, 1997. 971-1223.

Thiong'o, Ngũgĩ wa. *Globalectics: Theory and the Politics of Knowing*. Columbia U. Press, 2012.

Van Hooft, Stan. *Cosmopolitanism: A Philosophy for Global Ethics*. McGill-Queens U. Press, 2009.

Article 6:

Ask me once, stranger you; ask me twice, stranger me.

6.1: Poetry For Xenophilia

Bush, George W. *Executive Order.* http://www.whitehouse.gov/news/releases/2007/07/print/20070720-4.html

Camus, Albert. *The Stranger.* Trans. Matthew Ward. Vintage, 1989.

Casteel, Joshua. *Letters from Abu Ghraib.* Essay Press, 2008.

Kapil, Bhanu. *The Vertical Interrogation of Strangers.* Kelsey St. Press, 2001.

Rushdie, Salman. *Imaginary Homelands.* Granta Books, 1991.

6.2: Poetry For Change

Kapil, Bhanu. *The Vertical Interrogation of Strangers.* Kelsey St. Press, 2001.

LaMon, Jacqueline Jones. *Last Seen.* U. of Wisconsin Press, 2011.

Article 7:

No secrets means no exceptions.

7.1: Poetry Against Expectations

Aristotle. *Nicomachean Ethics.* In *The Basic Works of Aristotle.* Ed. Richard McKeon. Random House, 1941. 927-1112.

Berlant, Lauren. *Cruel Optimism.* Duke U. Press, 2011.

Carson, Anne. *Glass, Irony and God.* New Directions, 1995.

Dickinson, Emily. *The Complete Poems of Emily Dickinson.* Ed. Thomas H. Johnson. Little, Brown and Co., 1960.

Donne, John. *The Complete English Poems.* Ed. A. J. Smith. Penguin, 1971.

Holmes, Oliver Wendell. *The Poetical Works.* James R. Osgood and Co., 1877.

Homer. *The Iliad.* Trans. Robert Fagles. Penguin, 1990.

Jarrell, Randall. *Selected Poems.* Atheneum, 1980.

Kapil, Bhanu. *The Vertical Interrogation of Strangers.* Kelsey St. Press, 2001.

Mackey, Nathaniel. *Splay Anthem.* New Directions, 2006.

McHugh, Heather. *Hinge & Sign: Poems, 1968-1993.* Wesleyan U. Press, 1994.

Milton, John. *Complete Poems and Major Prose.* Ed. Merritt Y. Hughes. Odyssey Press, 1957.

Plath, Sylvia. *The Collected Poems.* Ed. Ted Hughes. Harper Perennial, 1992.

Rich, Adrienne. *Arts of the Possible: Essays and Conversations.* Norton, 2001.

Santos, Sherod. *A Poetry of Two Minds.* U. of Georgia Press, 2000.

Stevens, Wallace. *The Collected Poems.* Vintage, 1982.

Thayer, Phineas. *Casey at the Bat.* A. C. McClurg & Co., 1912.

Wright, C. D. *One Big Self: An Investigation.* Copper Canyon Press, 2007.

Wright, James. *Collected Poems.* Wesleyan U. Press, 1972.

7.2: Poetry Against Exceptionalism

Braidotti, Rosi. *The Posthuman.* Polity Press, 2013.

BLM website: http://www.blm.gov/wo/st/en/info/About_BLM.html

Carnegie, Andrew. *The Gospel of Wealth and Other Timely Essays.* Ed. Edward C. Kirkland. Harvard U. Press, 1962.

Coleridge, Samuel Taylor. *Biographia Literaria. Collected Works* 7:1. Ed. James Engell and W. Jackson Bate. Princeton U. Press, 1983.

Greenberg, Amy S. *Manifest Destiny and American Territorial Expansion: A Brief History with Documents.* Bedford/St. Martin's, 2012.

Kant, Immanuel. *Critique of Judgment.* Trans. J. H. Bernard. Hafner Press, 1951.

Merwin, W. S. *Collected Poems 1952-1993.* Ed. J. D. McClatchy. The Library of America, 2013.

Sartre, Jean-Paul. *Existentialism and Humanism.* Trans. Philip Mairet. Haskell House Publishers, 1948.

Shiva, Vandana. *Earth Democracy: Justice, Sustainability, and Peace.* South End Press, 2005.

Thoreau, Henry D. *Walden.* Ed. J. Lyndon Shanley. Princeton U. Press, 1971.

Wolfe, Cary. *What Is Posthumanism?* U. of Minnesota Press, 2010.

Article 8:
Tell me someone I don't already know.

8.1: Poetry For Discovery

Bloom, Harold. *The Anxiety of Influence: A Theory of Poetry*. Oxford U. Press, 1973.

Harrison, Robert Pogue. *The Dominion of the Dead*. U. of Chicago Press, 2003.

Latour, Bruno and Peter Weibel, eds. *Iconoclash: Beyond the Image Wars in Science, Religion, and Art*. MIT Press, 2002.

Osman, Jena. "Procedural Poetry: The Intentions of Nonintention." In *An Exaltation of Forms: Contemporary Poets Celebrate the Diversity of Their Art*. Ed. Annie Finch and Kathrine Varnes. U. of Michigan Press, 2002. 366-78.

8.2: Poetry For Self-Knowledge

Goldman, Francisco. "The Great Bolaño." *The New York Review of Books* 54:12 (19 July 2007), 34-37.

Article 9:
One word changes, one word changes everything.

9.1: Poetry Against Correspondence

Ahmed, Sara. *Willful Subjects*. Duke U. Press, 2014.

Dubreuil, Laurent. *The Intellective Space: Thinking beyond Cognition*. U. of Minnesota Press, 2015.

Gass, William H. *Fiction and the Figures of Life*. David R. Godine, 1978.

Hirsch, Edward. *A Poet's Glossary*. Houghton Mifflin Harcourt, 2014.

Hobbes, Thomas. *Leviathan*. Ed. C. B. Macpherson. Penguin, 1981.

Huntington, Samuel P. *The Clash of Civilizations and the Remaking of the World Order*. Simon & Schuster, 1996.

Kahn, Charles H. *The Art and Thought of Heraclitus*. Cambridge U. Press, 1979.

Kirk, G. S., and J. E. Raven. *The Presocratic Philosophers*. Cambridge U. Press, 1957.

Lakoff, George. *Women, Fire, and Dangerous Things: What Categories Reveal about the Mind*. U. of Chicago Press, 1987.

Meredith, William. "The Illiterate." *The Open Sea and Other Poems*. Alfred A. Knopf, 1958.

Preminger, Alex, and T. V. F. Brogan, eds. *The New Princeton Encyclopedia of Poetry and Poetics*. Princeton U. Press, 1993.

Scalapino, Leslie. *The Public World / Syntactically Impermanence*. Wesleyan U. Press, 1999.

Sen, Amartya. *Identity and Violence: The Illusion of Destiny*. W. W. Norton, 2006.

Wittgenstein, Ludwig. *Philosophical Investigations*. 3rd Ed. Trans. G. E. M. Anscombe. Macmillan, 1966.

Zwicky, Jan. *Alkibiades' Love: Essays in Philosophy*. McGill-Queens U. Press, 2015.

Zwicky, Jan. *Wisdom & Metaphor*. Gaspereau Press, 2003.

https://web.cn.edu/kwheeler/lit_terms_I.html.

http://en.wikipedia.org/wiki/Rhyme#Identical_rhymes.

http://english.stackexchange.com/questions/113778/why-are-identical-rhymes-inferior-in-english-poetry.

9.2: Poetry Against Fungibility

Blake, William. *The Complete Poetry and Prose of William Blake*. Rev. ed. Ed. David V. Erdman. Anchor Books, 1988.

Brooks, Gwendolyn. *Selected Poems*. Harper & Row, 1963.

Hayden, Robert. *Collected Poems*. Ed. Frederick Glaysher. Liveright, 1985.

Hejinian, Lyn. *The Language of Inquiry*. U. of California Press, 2000.

Lakoff, George. *Women, Fire, and Dangerous Things: What Categories Reveal about the Mind*. U. of Chicago Press, 1987.

Oppen, George. "Selections from George Oppen's Daybooks." *The Iowa Review* 18:3 (Fall 1988).

Szymborska, Wislawa. *Poems New and Collected: 1957-1997*. Trans. Stanislaw Baranczak and Clare Cavanagh. Harcourt, 1998.

Vera, Yvonne. *Butterfly Burning*. Farrar, Straus and Giroux, 2000.

Zwicky, Jan. *Wisdom & Metaphor*. Gaspereau Press, 2003.

Article 10:

Not yet as it should be, no longer as it was.

10.1: Poetry For Dissent

Bush, George W. "Remarks by the President at Mike Fisher for Governor Luncheon." 5 August 2002. http://www.whitehouse.gov/news/releases/2002/08/20020805-4.html

Havelock, Eric. *Preface to Plato.* Harvard U. Press, 1963.

Hietala, Thomas R. *Manifest Design: American Exceptionalism and Empire.* Rev. Ed. Cornell U. Press, 2003.

Joy, Mark S. *American Expansionism, 1783-1860.* Pearson Longman, 2003.

Melville, Herman. *Moby-Dick.* Ed. Hershel Parker and Harrison Hayford. W. W. Norton, 2002.

Merk, Frederick. *Manifest Destiny and Mission in American History: A Reinterpretation.* Alfred A. Knopf, 1963.

Metres, Philip. *Behind the Lines: War Resistance Poetry on the American Homefront Since 1941.* U. of Iowa Press, 2007.

O'Sullivan, John L. "Annexation." In *Manifest Destiny and the Imperialism Question.* Ed. Charles L. Sanford. John Wiley & Sons, 1974. 26-32.

10.2: Poetry For Hybridity

Bringhurst, Robert. *A Story as Sharp as a Knife: The Classical Haida Mythtellers and Their World.* U. of Nebraska Press, 2000.

Burke, Kenneth. *A Grammar of Motives.* U. of California Press, 1969.

Cixous, Hélène. *Three Steps on the Ladder of Writing.* Trans. Sarah Cornell and Susan Sellers. Columbia U. Press, 1993.

"Historical Estimates of World Population." U.S. Census Bureau. 5 June 2011.

Google Ngram Viewer. 5 June 2011.

Books from Etruscan Press

Zarathustra Must Die | Dorian Alexander
The Disappearance of Seth | Kazim Ali
Drift Ice | Jennifer Atkinson
Crow Man | Tom Bailey
Coronology | Claire Bateman
Topographies | Stephen Benz
What We Ask of Flesh | Remica L. Bingham
The Greatest Jewish-American Lover in Hungarian History | Michael Blumenthal
No Hurry | Michael Blumenthal
Choir of the Wells | Bruce Bond
Cinder | Bruce Bond
The Other Sky | Bruce Bond and Aron Wiesenfeld
Peal | Bruce Bond
Poems and Their Making: A Conversation | Moderated by Philip Brady
Crave: Sojourn of a Hungry Soul | Laurie Jean Cannady
Toucans in the Arctic | Scott Coffel
Sixteen | Auguste Corteau
Wattle & daub | Brian Coughlan
Body of a Dancer | Renée E. D'Aoust
Ill Angels | Dante Di Stefano
Aard-vark to Axolotl: Pictures From my Grandfather's Dictionary | Karen Donovan
Scything Grace | Sean Thomas Dougherty
Areas of Fog | Will Dowd
Romer | Robert Eastwood
Surrendering Oz | Bonnie Friedman
Nahoonkara | Peter Grandbois
The Candle: Poems of Our 20th Century Holocausts | William Heyen
The Confessions of Doc Williams & Other Poems | William Heyen
The Football Corporations | William Heyen
A Poetics of Hiroshima | William Heyen
September 11, 2001: American Writers Respond | Edited by William Heyen
Shoah Train | William Heyen
American Anger: An Evidentiary | H. L. Hix
As Easy As Lying | H. L. Hix
As Much As, If Not More Than | H. L. Hix
Chromatic | H. L. Hix
First Fire, Then Birds | H. L. Hix
God Bless | H. L. Hix
I'm Here to Learn to Dream in Your Language | H. L. Hix
Incident Light | H. L. Hix
Legible Heavens | H. L. Hix
Lines of Inquiry | H. L. Hix

Etruscan Press Is Proud of Support Received From

Wilkes University

Youngstown State University

The Raymond John Wean Foundation

The Ohio Arts Council

The Stephen & Jeryl Oristaglio Foundation

The Nathalie & James Andrews Foundation

The National Endowment for the Arts

The Ruth H. Beecher Foundation

The Bates-Manzano Fund

The New Mexico Community Foundation

Founded in 2001 with a generous grant from the Oristaglio Foundation, Etruscan Press is a nonprofit cooperative of poets and writers working to produce and promote books that nurture the dialogue among genres, achieve a distinctive voice, and reshape the literary and cultural histories of which we are a part.

etruscan press

www.etruscanpress.org

Etruscan Press books may be ordered from

Consortium Book Sales and Distribution
800.283.3572
www.cbsd.com

Etruscan Press is a 501(c)(3) nonprofit organization.
Contributions to Etruscan Press are tax deductible
as allowed under applicable law.
For more information, a prospectus,
or to order one of our titles,
contact us at books@etruscanpress.org.